DAYS AT THE RACES

Three Generations of the Day family, 1838.
(painted by Abraham Cooper, RA)
Anne Day with Mrs. John Barham Day in their mule carriage on Danebury Downs; John Barham Day (with whip) and John Day the third (both standing); Sam Day on Venison (centre) and his brother William Day on Chapeau d'Espagne, both wearing Lord George Bentinck's colours.
Tate, London 2006

Days at the Races

**A History of the Stockbridge Racecourse ......
and the Day and Cannon families that ran it.**

Anthony C. Raper

ANDOVER HISTORY & ARCHAEOLOGY SOCIETY
2006

DAYS AT THE RACES

Published by Andover History and Archaeology Society
c/o Andover Public Library
Chantry Way, Andover SP10 1LT.

ISBN: 0 903755 22 X

CONTENTS

Acknowledgements

Grateful thanks go to Derek Tempero and H.W. Earney for their help and allowing me to use their works and extensive knowledge of the area. Thanks to the staff of the Andover Library for their patience and finding me the obscure books I requested. Thanks also to June Harris for allowing me to quote from her article which appeared in the *Hampshire Magazine* in 1993 and to Greg Gregory for pointing me at other reference sources. Thanks also to Diana Coldicott, David Borrett and other members of the Andover History & Archaeology Society's publications sub-committee.

Tate Britain, the National Portrait Gallery and the Metropolitan Museum of New York have kindly given permission for their images to be used. Several images have been taken from *The Racehorse in Training* by William Day and Alfred J. Day.

ILLUSTRATIONS

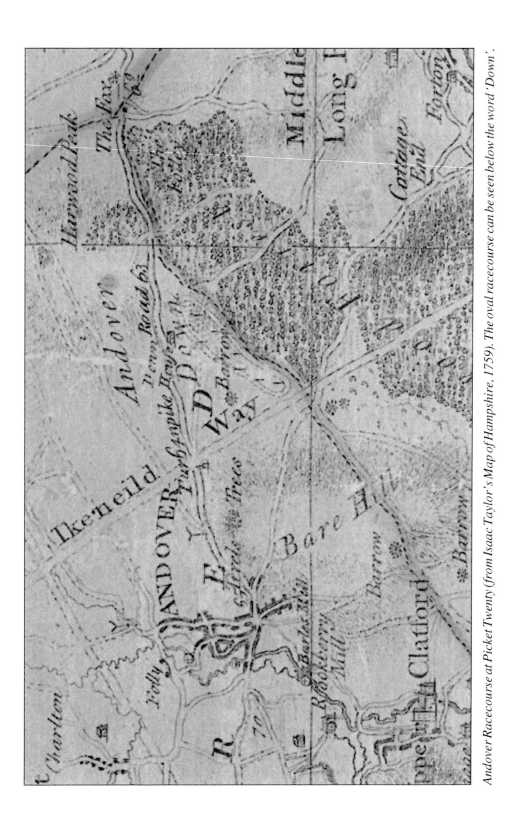

Andover Racecourse at Picket Twenty (from Isaac Taylor's Map of Hampshire, 1759). The oval racecourse can be seen below the word 'Down'.

CHAPTER ONE

RACING IN THE ANDOVER AND STOCKBRIDGE AREA

Horse racing has always been a popular sport in the Andover area and with so many local training establishments this is not surprising. Although the town never claimed to have an official racecourse, Isaac Taylor's 1759 map of Andover clearly shows a race-course on Andover Down, running alongside the Andover to Whitchurch road. Little more is known and it has for some time been considered as no more than a site where local owners matched their horses against each other as an ancillary entertainment to the prizefights held on a field behind the Queen Charlotte Inn in London Road.

Evidence is growing however that it was more than this, for reports in the *Salisbury Journal* and *Hampshire Chronicle* newspapers in the 1770s suggest it was a thriving local pastime. As always, gambling was part of the race proceedings and the newspapers revelled in reflecting popular feeling, especially if one of the bookmakers was on the losing side. One such incident took place at Andover Races in 1772 when a crowd were about to administer the usual judgement of a 'horsewhipping' against a 'bookie' or 'black legged gentry' who defaulted to pay out, when some of his fellows stepped in to pay the bet for him. After another race meeting in September 1775, there was a Grand Ball at the Star and Garter Hotel, Andover (now the Danebury Hotel), for which tickets were three shillings each and tea was "included".

Some of the patrons of this course were from famous racing families including the Craven family (from Hamstead Marshall, Berks.), Lord Portsmouth of Hurstbourne Priors, the Duke of Bolton (Winchester) and the Poulett family.[1] It is recorded that the second Duke of Cumberland had winners at Andover Races in 1777.[2] We have no dates for the closure of the Andover course.

For a short time in the 1840s the village of Hurstbourne Tarrant could boast its own race meeting. The last meet was in 1846, closing during a period when the social and economic climate was becoming hostile to the old style, local country racing.[3]

In 1892 the Andover Racing Club was formed and their inaugural meet was held at Weyhill under the National Pony and Galloway Racing Rules on July 19th and 20th that year. A newspaper advertisement survives showing that the meet was organised through the Weyhill Stables. Over the following years the meeting became known locally as the Penton Horse Races and was held on land adjacent to Foxcotte Lane, the road running from Charlton village to Weyhill. It was a very popular event with many marquees and bookmakers stands. The course extended from close to the Harroway and ran eastwards over jumps toward the Andover boundary, where it turned northward through the water, across Foxcotte Lane. It continued around a plantation known as the Gorse, at the lower end of Penton Park, southward back over

Foxcotte Lane and westward toward Weyhill Bottom. The first day's racing was commandeered by Cavalry Regiments from Tidworth with military bands playing almost constantly and the second day was mostly organised by the Tedworth Hunt. The racing was eventually moved to Larkhill.[4] More research is required on this event as records must exist in the local newspapers from the 1890s to the 1930s.

In addition to the Andover and Penton Horse Races, Salisbury had its own course which survives to this day and there were courses at Basingstoke (1737-1850), Marlborough (1730-1811 and 1840-1874), Chippenham (1808-1816), Lyndhurst (1859-1871), Broadhalfpenny Down (Hambledon), Winchester (1740-1887), Southampton (1804-1881) and Blandford.[5] In the early days of racing these meetings would have taken on a kind of carnival atmosphere with plenty of sideshows offering opportunities to gamble. These events included foot races for both men and women (sometimes known as smock-races), cudgelling contests and backsword contests as well as wrestling, football, cricket and even hunt meets. At some of these events, often in one of the many hostelries nearby, there were also such sports as cockfights, bear baiting and of course the inevitable prize fights.

The Stockbridge Racecourse

Stockbridge Racecourse was always associated with the local trainers, in particular the Day family, more of whom appear in another chapter. No one has been able to ascertain when horse racing actually began in the Stockbridge area, but it was probably held on the downs near Houghton Down Farm. First mention of the racecourse at Stockbridge occurs in 1735 and its reputation grew steadily over the following years. In 1742 Lord Byron, the Earl of Berkeley and Fulke Greville all appeared on the downs in a three-heat sweepstake riding their own horses.[6] The Prince of Wales in 1746 awarded a prize of 60 guineas "as a present to the town" and continued with it until his death in 1751. Isaac Taylor's 1759 map provides further evidence of its existence. By 1775 the Stockbridge Races at Danebury were extremely popular with the country nobility and the Andover gentry.

Danebury was considered an essential place to be seen and no more so than in 1780 when the Prince of Wales (later Prince Regent) personally attended the Stockbridge Races. In the early days of the course, the horses were entered and shown at The Swan Inn in the High Street, now occupied by Lane Antiques. It was not unknown for the programme at The Swan to include prize fighting and cockfights. Many local families found that by renting out their homes at the times of the races they could earn sufficient money to pay their rent for the rest of the year.

John Day of Houghton Farm (later Danebury) was Clerk of the Course and a portrait exists, painted by Harry Hill in 1826, of him on his favourite cob, *Black Jack*, with Danebury Hill and the Stockbridge Racecourse in the distance. On one occasion a local sporting parson came up to John saying "Mr. Day, my daughter is in the stand,

A portrait of John Day (Gloomy Day) on Black Jack.
(from a watercolour by Harry Hill, 1826)

and there is a naughty lady there. Will you have her removed?" John Day bought his 21 stone erect and hardly daring to smile replied "A naughty Lady! I have never seen such a thing in my life. Do show her to me". No record exists of the outcome to this story, but he was known as a tactful person and we assume he acted with diplomacy and found the solution.[7]

Andover and Stockbridge were without a local newspaper during the early years of the 19th century so reports of events at the races were recorded in the *Salisbury & Winchester Journal*. Two reports of early meetings at Stockbridge can be found dated Monday, 27 June 1825 which gives the winners of the 50 Guineas Sweepstakes and Coronation Stakes:

50 Guineas Sweepstakes
1. Mr Shard's b.c. *Hugumont* (J. Day)
2. Mr Wadhan Wyndham ch.c. by *Granicus*
3. Lord Grosvenor's *Achillies*

Coronation Stakes 25 sovereigns
1. Lord Palmerston's ch.c. *Grey-leg* (J. Day)
2. Lord Grosvenor's *Achillies*

In another report dated Monday, 25 June 1827, it states:

> At Stockbridge Races on Wednesday, Mr Radclyffe's *Windermere* walked over for the Sweepstakes of 50gs each, h. ft. for which 12 horses were entered. –
> Mr Gauntlett's *Gamelius* received forfeit in a match against Mr. Shard's *Dominie*. – There was no race for the Coronation Stakes, or for the 25 sovs. Sweepstakes for Colts – The Stockbridge Market Cup was won after 3 severe heats, by Mr Habbatt's c.g. The contest for the Cup afforded great sport and gratification to the company, who were very numerous and highly respectable. Mr Wilbraham is appointed Steward for the next year; when the Earl of Grosvenor will give a plate.

The Bibury Club

The popularity of Stockbridge Racecourse increased greatly after 1831 when the Bibury Club, the oldest racing club in England (it had been started in 1676 holding its first meeting in 1681 in Gloucestershire) transferred its races from Burford Downs to Danebury Downs near Stockbridge. The Bibury Club and Stockbridge Races were an annual meeting held in late June. As late as 1859, the Bibury Club had its headquarters in Andover at the Star and Garter Hotel. The club eventually transferred its headquarters to the Grosvenor Hotel in Stockbridge, where a small collection of racing memorabilia can still be seen. Under the influence of the Bibury Club, the racecourse was extended to 3 miles (24 furlongs) with new starting posts, giving the possibility of running one-mile races. The new race-goers enclosure boasted the jockeys' stand, the grandstand and the Bibury Club stand.

Several locally trained horses went on to win the Derby and some of the local houses nearby were named after Derby and Classics winners.

It was to the Market Room of the Grosvenor Hotel, which in the early 19th century was known as The King's Head, that the 'gentlemen riders', owners and jockeys would throng during race meetings. During race-weeks the area was bursting with visitors, traps, carriages and four-in-hands with their postillions, all going to the races. The inns of Andover, Stockbridge, Wallop and the local villages all did a brisk trade. Before the days of the railways, stage coaches and post coaches were the most expeditious means of travelling to and from the meeting, although the cost, at two shillings a mile, was by no means cheap.

Grosvenor Hotel, Stockbridge photographed in 1947. The hotel was owned by both the Day and Cannon families.

The Arrival of the Railway

The L&SWR railway (later known by the nickname 'The Sprat and Winkle') arrived in 1865 and the station at Stockbridge had special sidings built for the racehorse traffic to and from the stables at Danebury and Chattis Hill; these sidings survived until around 1910. With the nearby stations at Andover and Fullerton, the locals and 'city folk' had easy access to the racecourse. It also gave race-goers the opportunity to stay in the nearby towns of Romsey and Southampton, directly on the railway's route. (The Andover to Southampton line was another of those that fell under the axe of Dr. Beeching in 1964.)

By 1870 the *Andover Advertiser* newspaper was reporting that the numbers of race goers who were staying overnight in Andover was in decline:

> ......Those palmy days for the innkeepers and others have gone for ever, as the railway provides the sporting community with a direct route. So great was the demand for accommodation once, that almost fabulous prices were asked and paid, but this week's has been in excess of demand.

No doubt the real reason for this was the weather; that June was rainy and kept all but the determined race-goer from the turf. The report continues with a discussion on how life was during race week in Andover:

......An importation of cabs were ready to convey passengers to and from the course. In the evenings, large crowds of boys were diverted in front of the hotels by the visitors throwing coppers out of the window, and then a paper bag, filled with flour, was sent into their midst, transforming some unlucky youth into a miller.[8]

The Prince of Wales attended the races that year, arriving at Andover Junction Station before travelling on to stay at a friend's house in Stockbridge. That friend was John Barham Day and the house in question was Danebury House, a mere stone's throw from the racecourse.

An amusement associated with the races at Stockbridge in the late 18th century was held in the local pubs in the village, as the following notice for a cock-fighting meeting shows:

Cocking at Stockbridge. A regular main of cocks to be fought during the races, the 6th, 7th and 8th of July near the "Swan", Stockbridge, between the gentlemen of Winchester and Andover for 5 guineas a battle and twenty the odd. To begin fighting each day at 12 o'clock.

A 'Main' consisted of any number of cocks between seven and forty, and the money went to the owner of the bird which won the most fights. It was not until 1835 that an Act of Parliament was able to declare cock fighting as a cruel sport, which gambling alone had succeeded in keeping alive. It was abolished in 1849 but since then has continued illegally as an 'underground' sport.

By 1859 there were two racehorse-training establishments in the area belonging to Mr Young King of Stockbridge and Mr John B. Day of Danebury. These were held in high repute. White's 1859 *Directory* alludes to another racecourse and tells us that the "Houghton Down Stables and Race Course are closed". The Bibury Club and Stockbridge Races held on the downs near Danebury Hill, on the third Wednesday and Thursday in June, attracted large crowds and visitors to witness the races. The largest field ever recorded at Stockbridge was for the Amport Stakes of 1860, which was run over a mile and a half, when twenty one riders turned out.

One of the country's most famous jockeys during the nineteenth century was Fred Archer and whilst attending Stockbridge Races he would stay with his great friend Billy Moon, a local benefactor and eccentric, at Penton Lodge in Penton Mewsey near Andover.

A sale poster survives, albeit in a poor state, describing an auction and the rights to sell refreshments and to run the parking franchise at Stockbridge race meetings. Note the high charges for parking carriages and coaches on the racing enclosure:

John Barham Day (from a miniature)

STOCKBRIDGE RACES
17th. 18th 19th JUNE 1863

To INNKEEPERS & Others:

TO BE LET, By Auction, by Mr. F. ELLEN,

At the GRANDSTAND, on Stockbridge Race Course,
On Tuesday, JUNE 9th, 1863, at two o'clock in the afternoon

1. The right of serving Refreshments in the Grandstand during the three days Races.

2. The whole of the Ground between the Betting Enclosure and the Road, except a certain space near the Grand Stand and sufficient approaches thereto, which will be reserved for Carriages setting down and taking up at the Grand Stand. The highest bidder for this Lot will have the privilege of charging for all Vehicles entering upon the ground let to him at a rate not exceeding 3s. for each Coach, Omnibus, Van, Break, Landau, Britzka, four-

wheel Cab, Chariot, or Fly; 2s. for each ordinary four-wheel Phaeton, and 1s. each for two-wheel Vehicles.

He will also be entitled to underlet the ground for Snuff-boxing Sticks &c.

(Snuff-boxing sticks were walking sticks with snuff-boxes carved into their handles.)

The National Gazetteer in 1868 describes the town of Stockbridge giving us a general feeling of a quiet small country town, which came to life in June each year for the races..

STOCKBRIDGE, a parish, post, and market town in the upper division of Thorngate hundred, having separate jurisdiction, but locally in county Hants, 9 miles N. of Romsey, and 9 N. W. of Winchester. It is a station on the Andover and Southampton branch of the London and South-Western railway. It is situated on the river Test and the Andover and Redbridge canal, the former being celebrated for its trout fishing. It is a petty sessions town, and until disfranchised by the Reform bill returned two members to Parliament. The town consists of one long street, forming part of the great western road, with the town hall standing nearly in the centre. There were formerly numerous small bridges over the branches of the Test, which intersect the main street, but these have recently been taken down except one, and the whole has been arched over.

In this parish are the union poorhouse and a police station, also two extensive training establishments for race horses. The Houghton Fishing Club is held at the Grosvenor Arms, which is also used by the members of the Bibury Racing Club, removed hither from Gloucestershire. The preparation of parchment and glue afford employment to a few persons, but the chief business is in agricultural produce. The living is a rectory in the diocese of Winchester, value £198. The church, dedicated to St. Peter, is an ancient edifice, with a tower containing four bells. There is a parochial school. The Independents have a chapel. The race-stand is situated near Danebury-hill camp, under which is the course, recently formed in the adjoining parishes of Wallop and Longstock. Lord Clarendon is lord of the manor. Market day is on Thursday. A fair for the sale of lambs is held on 10th July. The races are in June.

Stockbridge was considered amongst the finest of the provincial racecourses and few fixtures were more keenly anticipated than the three days in summer on the downs at Danebury. In June 1869 the *Andover Advertiser* report reported that the Bibury Club Meeting at Stockbridge was well attended and listed a number of aristocrats being present including the Duke of Beaufort, the Marquis of Anglesey, Lords Suffolk, Royston, Stamford, Westmoreland, Durham, Portsmouth, Vivian, Calthorpe, Count Batthany, Sir F. Johnstone, Sir Watkin Wynne, Sir C. Legend, Mr Crawford, Sir Robert Peel, Mr Saville and Prince Soltykoff among others.

The Hurstbourne Cup Stakes, established in 1870 at Lord Portsmouth's suggestion, was a two and a half mile race with a prize valued at 200 sovereigns and an additional sweepstake prize of 15 guineas. It replaced the earlier Hurstbourne Plate, donated personally by Lord Portsmouth and was worth 50 sovereigns to the winner. The Stockbridge Cup Stakes came next in importance; the cup was a fine piece of plate valued at 300 sovereigns.

The Stockbridge Cup

The Duke of Beaufort, Lord Anglesey and Lord Hastings were very frequent visitors and their patronage kept the Danebury horseboxes full. Another prominent race-goer was Lord Palmerston, Prime Minister for periods in the 1850s and 60s, who lived at Broadlands in Romsey, more recently the home of the Mountbatten family. The course was not just confined to gentlemen for it was not unusual for ladies also to frequent race days. One of Stockbridge's most prominent patrons was Lady Bampfylde, a racehorse owner. Often these ladies raced under their husband's or an assumed name so as not to draw scorn upon themselves.[9]

There were two grandstands, one for the use of the general public, built by John Day in 1831, and the other built by private subscription from a fund begun in 1866 by Colonel John Astley (later Sir John) that was the property of the Bibury Club. The new stand, opened in 1867, was a fine building which replaced earlier wooden stands. At some stage, a starting gate invented by Thomas Marshall was installed. The course became a major centre for racing and was described in racing circles as "there is so much space, and such is the conformation of the ground, that, from the fall of the flag you shall behold, not, as is usually the case, your neighbour's hat, or the fringe of a lady's parasol, but every change and incident of the contest to the final struggle out of the treacherous dip to the winning-post."[10]

The *Andover Advertiser* reported in 1870 that:

Last year the Prince of Wales honoured this old established club with his presence, this year Prince Teck was present. The Stockbridge (still increasing and "A1") meeting will probably equal some day the first in the kingdom, and standing as it does now in the first rank for two-year-old races. The races this year have been good and the attendance large.

The races created problems for the local schools as the following references from the logbooks of Houghton School indicate:

- 22nd June 1871 "Rather low school in consequence of the Stockbridge Races".
- 28th June 1872 "..owing to the Stockbridge Races … there has been a small attendance".

The Jockey Club in the early 1870s was making intensive efforts to stamp out corruption on racecourses and was taking the first steps to limit races over the shortest distances with the youngest horses and lightest weights. New regulations also began to impose minimum levels of prize money for individual races and race days. Over the next few years the number of race meetings declined and decisions taken in 1885 further reduced the number of racecourses on which the Royal Plates could be held from fourteen down to ten, including Bath and Stockbridge, which had never featured a Royal Plate before. The regulations also raised their prize money to 300 guineas per race and restricted entry to horses bred in Great Britain and Ireland. It is interesting to note that the Prince of Wales had been elected to the Jockey Club in 1864 and began racing horses under his own royal colours during the 1870s. It has been suggested that as many of his closest friends were prominent members of the Club that he had a personal interest in the disbursement of the 'Royal Bounty'.

It was not until 1870 that the electric telegraph was installed at Stockbridge racecourse; until that time the race results trickled out by word of mouth, with mail-coach drivers being the key transmitters. For some of the bigger meetings pigeons and sometimes trail-trained hounds carried the news. This must have greatly reduced the opportunity for those in the know to cheat the unsuspecting.[11]

The following extract from the *Illustrated London News*, dated July 1st 1882, page 10 is reproduced in its entirety below:

A Tuesday without racing is, indeed, a remarkable phenomenon in the height of the season, but last week no meeting began until the Wednesday, which was devoted to the Bibury Club gathering. The Champagne Stakes, in which Lord Falmouth introduced us to *Britomartis*, was the principal event of the day. She is a fine-looking daughter of *Wild Oats* and *Nike*, and is the first of his present batch of two-year-olds that has yet appeared in public. It did not seem that much was thought of her at home, and, for once, the public quite neglected Archer, who actually started at the nice price of 10 to 1, and won easily. *Madrid*, who was favourite, could only get third, and her 7lb. penalty kept *Lovely* out of a place. *St. Blaise*, a chestnut colt by *Hermit-Fusee*, who had a great private reputation, made his debut in the Twenty-fourth Biennial Stakes, and had no trouble in beating *The Duke* and three others. The first day of the Stockbridge Meeting, usually one of the pleasantest fixtures of the season, was completely ruined by a continuous downpour of rain, and everyone was thankful when the card was run through. Good odds were laid on the handsome *Beau Brummel* for the Mottisfont Stakes, and they might have been landed pretty easily had he not broken down in the course of the race, which enabled the *Cremorne-Hetty* colt to defeat him by a neck. *Sigmophone*, whose previous performances had been disappointing, secured the Stockbridge Cup from *Mowerina*, *Althotas*, and three others, all older than himself, and, though a difficult colt to ride, he was beautifully handled by little Martin. On the Friday *Geheimniss* was an absentee from the Twenty-third Biennial Stakes, so *Laureate* had really nothing to beat. The meeting of *Petronel* and *Wolseley* in the Queen's Plate excited considerable interest, and, at last, there was nothing to choose between them in the betting. The result was quite in accordance with the market, as the finish was a desperate one, and it was only in the last stride or two that Archer managed to win on *Petronel* by the shortest of heads. The field for the valuable Hurstbourne Stakes was remarkably select, if not very numerous, as *Adriana*, *St. Blaise*, and *Tyndrum* had all secured winning brackets, and the "dark" colt by *Macaroni* from *Heather Bell* came out with a great flourish of trumpets, being reputed many pounds in front of the *Hetty* colt. After her brilliant race at Ascot, in which she decisively cut down the previously undefeated *Rookery*, backers seemed quite justified in laying 6 to 4 on *Adriana* who, however, was completely out of it before reaching the distance, and the *Heather Bell* colt won in such easy fashion that, though his forelegs do not look particularly sound, an offer of 1000 to 100 against him for next year's Derby was promptly accepted, and, so far, he is undoubtedly the crack of his year.

In 1886 a racing correspondent in *The Daily News*, wrote of Stockbridge "… many sportsmen regard the three days spent here as among the pleasantest of the whole season. The racing is always of good quality, without any of the bustle and excitement attending such meetings as Epsom, Ascot and Goodwood; and if pleasant weather is accorded, the sport will be most enjoyable."

William Day recalls in his book *Turf Celebrities I have Known* that ".. I once saw a horse jump the chains at Stockbridge, which might have killed the horse or the rider, as it did poor Connolly, a very favourite jockey, at Oxford, his horse falling over the chains with such terrific force it killed him."

An article written anonymously by someone calling himself 'Borderer' about the "English Race Courses" and published in 1900 (but obviously written earlier) describes Stockbridge as "a grand course, with all the telling severity of a gentle ascent right up to the winning chair – so much so that the good judges love to see a two year old run over it". It mentions that it is the home of the "oldest racing club, next to the Jockey Club – the favourite trysting ground for our gentlemen jocks." The article continues, mentioning the "celebrated training ground of Danebury" and its "excellent and deserving master, Tom Cannon."[12]

Clerks of the Course – Stockbridge

Mr. Wilbraham	1827 - 1828
John Day ('Gloomy Day')	1828 - 1829
John Barham Day	1829 - 1860
John Day	1860 - 1882
Tom Cannon	1883 - 1898 [closure].

CHAPTER TWO

STOCKBRIDGE RACES IN VICTORIAN TIMES

The Prince of Wales, later King Edward VII, visited the Stockbridge Races often and he was there in 1886 when his horse *Counterpane*, entered in the Stockbridge Cup, put up a disappointing performance only to fall and die shortly after passing the winning post in last place. It was said that souvenir hunters pulled out every hair of the horse's tail.

Edward, when he was Prince of Wales, often stayed at Danebury House as the guest of Tom Cannon or if in Stockbridge he stayed at Hermit Lodge in the Houghton Road during meetings; a footbridge over the river links the garden of this house with that of nearby Grosvenor House. Edward also stayed occasionally at Amport House as a guest of the sixteenth Marquis of Winchester and whilst there took in the Stockbridge Races and his other passion, partridge shooting.

Edward, Prince of Wales was a frequent visitor to Stockbridge Races.

Lily Langtry, mistress of the Prince of Wales, often accompanied him.

Lily Langtry, the Prince's mistress, was often seen with him at Stockbridge and on occasion stayed at Grosvenor House, now the White House in the High Street. Lily was a woman of considerable beauty but of no means. She had come to London in 1876 and in little over a year had become a celebrity, invited by prominent hostesses because her presence attracted other guests. Her face was on picture postcards and she was recognised wherever she went. The Prince of Wales was 'taken' with her and they were seen everywhere together, although their relationship only lasted three years. Her visits left a lasting impression on Stockbridge and Stockbridge Races remained in her memory. Her later career as an actress was less notorious but it enabled her to achieve independence and a comfortable fortune. She went on to own a successful racing stable in Newmarket and won a number of notable races including the Cesarewitch, Ascot Gold Cup, Jockey Club Cup and the Goodwood Cup with her famous *Merman*. There are no records of any racing successes at Stockbridge.

Notable horses at Stockbridge Races included *Galtree mare* making her first appearance in the Hurstbourne Stakes in 1896 and later becoming one of the select band of Triple Crown winners. At the same meeting, the Prince of Wales won the Andover Stakes on *Safety Pin* and the All Aged Plate with *Courtier*.

Many farmers and local gentry boosted their income at race meetings by renting their houses to dignitaries, as in 1886 when Lord Warwick and the Greville family leased the home of J. Ernest Pain of Westover for the duration of the meeting.[13]

The Last Races

The landowner Sir John Barker Mill, who owned part of the land over which the racecourse ran, had died in 1860 leaving his estate to be administered by his widow until her own death in 1884. The inheritance then passed to a distant cousin, Marianne Vaudrey (who in 1903 added Barker-Mill to her surname). She was strongly disapproving of Sir John's gaming, racing and betting ways and vowed to correct some of the wrongs he had done. On the estate at Mottisfont, she handed all the pubs over to the "People's Refreshment Association", which sold food rather than alcohol, in the belief that drinking led to vice.[14]

In 1894 Marianne Vaudrey brought a trespass suit (under the Commons Act, 1876) against Tom Cannon "for unlawfully training horses and playing cricket and other games on his property". Tom Cannon answered the suit by asserting that the residents of Stockbridge had a right of recreation over the area and by "special custom" a further right to train racehorses on it. Mr. Justice Wright upheld the recreation claim, declaring that "the inhabitants of Stockbridge had from a remote period of time enjoyed the right to use the down for the purpose of playing cricket and other games."

The judge, however, denied the claim of a special custom to train race horses, revealing not only the courts' solicitude for rights of recreation but also a corresponding inclination to disallow claims to pursue commercial activities. It seems that even though Stockbridge had been a racing centre for over a century, and witnesses had testified to the absence of any previous interference with trainers who used the down, the judge rejected the notion of a special custom, declaring that the defendant's assertion was "too wide" .

The judge also prohibited Tom Cannon from removing a fence but directed the conservators to allow the defendant "access for commonable beasts at suitable times and seasons". In actual fact such an order was meaningless in practice because Mr Cannon had no commonable beasts on the land, and indeed no other person had objected to the fence. The judge decided that Marianne Vaudrey's assertion was "too wide", because trainers not normally resident in the parish also used the down for this purpose. The case was therefore rejected on a technicality that a landowner could not prevent a local inhabitant from riding a horse for recreation on the down but could preclude a professional trainer from using the same land to further business interests. He declined to judge whether an inhabitant of the borough who was not a professional racehorse trainer was entitled to train his own horses.[15]

This case then gave rise to fears throughout the racing fraternity that the 'lady' wanted the racecourse off her land and would do almost anything to ensure its closure. At the 1897 meeting, a 'heavy air' hung over the course with rumours that the Stockbridge meeting was likely to be abolished. It turned out to be true as the demise of Stockbridge Racecourse occurred the following year (1898) when the new owner, Marianne Vaudrey, in an attempt to curtail gambling, decided to withdraw the lease on both the racecourse and training ground after the June race meeting. This included the first two furlongs of the straight, five-furlong course and the finishing straight. Following this decision, the Bibury Club, the major sponsors of the racecourse, had no choice but to move its meetings to Salisbury Racecourse, where they are still held annually in July. Even today, the Bibury Meeting remains the most important meeting of the year at the Salisbury Racecourse.

The Jockey Club insisted that all racecourses should include a straight mile but with the shortening of the course it was no longer possible to have one at Stockbridge. This and the Bibury Club's move sealed the fate of the Stockbridge Racecourse and it subsequently closed, to the consternation of the locals and the betting fraternity.

A tenant farmer on Mrs Vaudrey Barker-Mill's estate told this tale about the event:

> She had to give notice to the club that she was going to sell it, and the Prince of Wales, afterwards King Edward VII, sent an equerry down there, with an open cheque to buy Stockbridge racecourse. But she tore it up and threw it in the fire. There's a strong-willed woman..... But she said afterwards that had she known the harm it had done Stockbridge, she wouldn't have closed it. It brought a tremendous income into Stockbridge; a lot of people in those three days' racing made enough to last a year.[16]

The *Andover Advertiser* printed this report on the last ever race meeting held at Stockbridge:

21

Races – During the week the town has again been the scene of bustle and life such as is only to be seen here in one week of the year, and this, according to current reports, will not occur again, this being the last meeting on the famous Danebury Downs.

Various are of the opinions expressed as to the future results to the town occasioned by loss of visitors at this season; but one thing is certain – that not only tradespeople but others will miss the ready cash which they have been accustomed to pocket during "race week". From what we hear most of the larger private houses have been let, and the hotels, etc., have been full during the week.

Vehicles of all descriptions plying for hire to and from the Down have been as numerous as ever, and seem to have done a good trade, especially on Wednesday, when the trains brought in a great number of people. Up to the time of writing the visitors have been most orderly, and during the evenings none of the disorderly scenes that were common years ago have been observed.

The arrangements made by the district council for watering the streets have been a great improvement on those of last year.

The *Andover Advertiser* concluded the article with the simple ending which says it all:

"So came to an end a colourful era of Stockbridge's ancient history."[17]

A photograph exists taken shortly before the third race, the Wallop Selling Plate (Handicap), on the last ever day's racing at Stockbridge 7th July 1898 showing the Bibury Club grandstand and the members' enclosure.

The closure was a major blow to Stockbridge and the local economy; it affected the profits in many of the local inns and hotels for miles around. The training of racing horses has however continued at Danebury, Houghton Down Farm and at the nearby Chattis Hill Stables.

One of the last events that were held in the Victorian Grandstand was the Coronation Supper Dance held on 23rd June 1902 to celebrate Edward VII's accession to the throne. A very fine menu was provided which included salmon, lobsters, beef and veal to be followed by Tipsy Cake etc. Miss Bennett of Andover and a pianist Mr Rovendio, also from Andover, provided the evening entertainment. Dancing continued throughout the night until six the next morning with the last carriages arriving at seven o'clock.

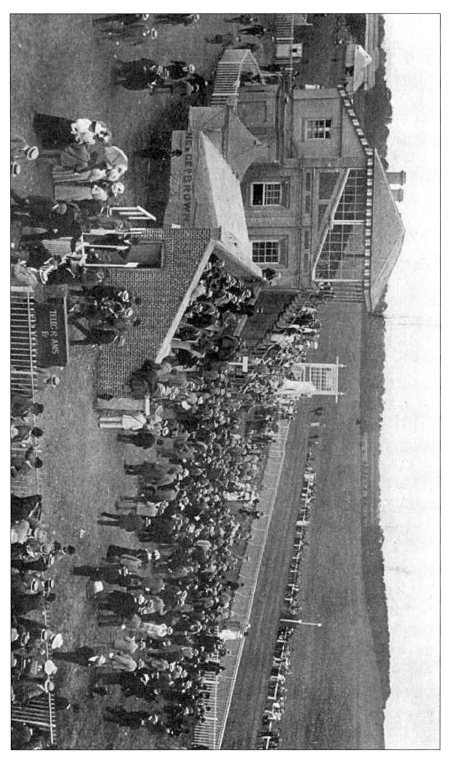

The last meeting at Stockbridge racecourse, 7th July 1898.

23

A Foolhardy Event marred the last Meeting

A sad event occurred at the last meeting when Charles Davies, a coal dealer of New Street, Andover was injured whilst trying to cross the course to get a better view from the other side. He later died in the Andover Cottage Hospital from the extensive wounds he sustained after he ran in front of a horse on the track.

"Lardy" as he was affectionately known, had just driven a party from Andover to the racecourse and had been warned off the course whilst the horses were making their parade. He attempted the same thing again prior to the second race and a police constable took him by the arm and put him back under the rail but, as the policeman turned his back, Davies dived under the rail and found himself in front of a galloping racehorse with nowhere to go. The horse shied at him and kicked out, striking him full force on the head and fracturing his skull. A doctor was called and did what he could for the poor man, but he immediately directed his removal to hospital. A collection was made on the racecourse and almost £200 was raised and passed on to his widow and four children.

Ipso facto gentlemen riders

In an article entitled "Race Courses For Thorough Bred Horses", which was originally published in 1898 as news of the imminent closure was on people's minds, there is the following description of Stockbridge Racecourse:

> One of the most popular of the few "open courses," as opposed to gate money meetings, which still remain, is at Stockbridge, the headquarters of the Bibury Club, one of the oldest established racing clubs in the country, members of which are ipso facto gentlemen riders, the only other English racing clubs which confer this distinction being the Jockey Club, Croxton Park, Southdown and Ludlow. Besides races for gentlemen riders Stockbridge, situated on the Downs near the historical training establishment of Danebury, has usually some very good two-year-old sport. The place has long been specially popular with many of the leading patrons of the turf, and it is seldom that good horses do not go to the post for the Hurstbourne Stakes— Stockbridge indeed is recognised as having a charm of its own, and much regret has been expressed at the report that a renewal of the lease for the training ground and racecourse cannot be obtained. It was here that the Marquis of Hastings and the Duke of Beaufort had their horses under the charge of John Day, father-in-law of the present tenant, Tom Cannon, during a very sensational period of turf history.

Memories of the Bibury Club at Stockbridge

Another of the late 19th/early 20th century trainers, Arthur Yates, wrote in 1921:

> Soon after I began race-riding I became a member of the Bibury Club, and have many happy memories of the old Stockbridge race-course. I believe I am right in saying that Viscount Chaplin and I are the only members surviving from those early days. Prominent members at that time were Captain Machell and the ill-fated Marquis of Hastings both of whom I knew well.

Captain James Octavia Machell (1837-1902) was a well respected and perhaps the most knowledgeable racing figure of the 19th century; he won hundreds of races, acting as racing manager to the Victorian elite. Captain Machell was a frequent visitor to Stockbridge and often rode there, but he is better known for his shrewd business deals. He died, aged 62, in 1902, a respected and wealthy man, having made a lot of money for other people. A good example of how he used his skills happened at the Bibury Club meeting at Stockbridge Racecourse on Wednesday 27th June 1877. The third race of the day was an All Aged selling plate, where the winner was to be sold for £100. *Alfred the Great*, a two-year-old colt owned by Mr Bignell, at 10 to 1, beat the short odds favourite *Cats Eyes* by two clear lengths and at the post-race auction Captain Machell purchased the horse at two hundred and thirty guineas. At the Stockbridge meeting, the following day, there was a race with the same conditions as the previous day and nine horses lined up for another All Aged plate. *Alfred the Great* ran in the colours of Mr H. Bird and dead-heated with *Curatrix*. In a run-off *Alfred the Great* won by a length and a half. At the resulting auction Capt. Machell sold the colt for six hundred guineas.

Viscount Henry Chaplin (1841-1923) was the 1st Viscount Chaplin, a racehorse owner and compulsive gambler. In 1866 he bought a horse, *Hermit*, with a view to entering him in one of the following year's racing classics, the Derby Stakes. Just ten days before the big race at the regulation trial, *Hermit* pulled up with a burst blood vessel. Chaplin was advised to withdraw from the Derby and the jockey, Custance, who was to have ridden him, was given another ride. *Hermit's* condition was found not to be serious and his trainer nursed him back to health, although he was not at peak condition on race day. Nobody paid him much attention but *Hermit* showed his mettle and came through winning by a neck in a late run.

The Marquis of Hastings was an owner of racehorses at the establishment of Henry Padwick, a moneylender, in the 1860s. This was at Downs House, Findon in West Sussex, a stables run by another John Day. A habitual gambler and drinker, the Marquis was an unpopular character and was frequently in the company of Padwick, a notorious swindler. It was Padwick who advised the Marquis to lay down a large bet against *Hermit* winning the Derby. Needless to say the Marquis lost heavily and never recovered – he died soon after the race, in 1867.

A Tale from the Racecourse

Hampshire is famous for its tales and there is one involving Stockbridge Racecourse. After arriving in Farnham to be interviewed for a clerical position a candidate was informed that the official who should have examined him had gone off to the Stockbridge Races. The candidate, not wishing to lose the opportunity of work, followed the official and cornered him in the paddock where the interview was completed. A Greek Testament was produced and the examination proceeded between the races, with the finale being, "All right, all right, you'll do! Now what will you put on in the next race?"[18]

All that is left are memories and ghosts

Miss Rosalind Hill, lady of the manor of Stockbridge and a local historian, recorded in a booklet *A Short History of Stockbridge and its Churches* written in 1963 that before the First World War, part of the old grandstand, the remains of which are still visible, was used as a Roman Catholic chapel for Stockbridge.

In their heyday the stables gave employment to farriers, smiths, saddlers and stable boys. Many local residents remember seeing strings of horses on their way to and from the railway station at Stockbridge. One resident, Monica Harding, recalled that a train was often delayed in its departure because a horse was reluctant to be loaded, making pupils late for school in Andover. At one time there were no fewer than nine racing stables in the Stockbridge area.

At the height of its use the course was one of the most important in the country and on a par with Newbury today. A fire in 1973 destroyed much of the old Bibury Club grandstand. However the ivy clad remnants, standing on private land, are still visible but the roof has collapsed in and is now in a highly dangerous condition. For a short while it was used for storing hay and straw. It seems sad that this shell of a building is all that is left save for the spirits and ghosts of many a nobleman of yesteryear.

The racecourse itself is now grazing pasture for sheep and remains a gallops for the nearby Danebury Stables. Interesting as it may be, it is not possible to visit the site.

In 1974 the popular BBC Radio 4 programme "Down Your Way" visited Stockbridge and interviewed the late Maurice Jones, who farmed the land which formed the old course.

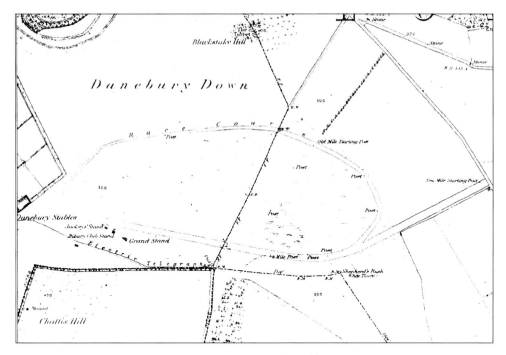

Ordnance Survey map of 1876 showing the site of Stockbridge Racecourse.

CHAPTER THREE

THE DAY FAMILY AND RACING SUCCESS

The Day family have a long association with Stockbridge Races and have been training horses in this area from the late 18th century. The chronology of the Day family is a little difficult to determine for there were three John Days (grandfather, father and son), two Samuels, two Alfreds, and two Williams. The first John Day was a large man tipping the scales at some 18 stones and nicknamed "Gloomy Day", even though he was reputed to be a cheerful sort of character. He began the family tradition of training racehorses and in 1790 married Anne Barham at Stockbridge.

In 1809 John Day took a lease on the Down Farm at Houghton, where he brought up six sons all of whom became jockeys. The Houghton Down stables were quite small, but were only about a mile from the racecourse where John was Clerk of the Course and played the primary roll in bringing the course up to its place of importance in the racing calendar. Among his associates was the Prince Regent, later King George IV, who described John as a 'jolly sort of fellow' and referred to him after consuming two bottles of wine as 'Lord Cinque Port', a title which he jokingly promised to confer on him when he became king. John died at the age of 62 in 1829. The caricature of John Day below was made at Brighton by Charles Dighton in 1801.

John Day (1767-1829) at Brighton, 1801.
(caricature by Charles Dighton)

Anne Day was not the little lady indoors, she was well known in racing circles as an opinionated woman who could hold her own in any argument with a man. She helped train the horses and followed the stable lads around to ensure they had cleared out the bins and done their jobs correctly. She was for a while Lady President of the Royal Veterinary College. Her trade mark was her black crunch bonnet and a thick walking stick. Abraham Cooper, R.A. painted her wearing that bonnet.

Anne Day, wife of John 'Gloomy' Day.
(painted by Abraham Cooper, RA)

Another painting of the Day family shows Mrs Anne Day and her daughter-in-law (J.B. Day's wife) sitting in a mule carriage with John Barham Day standing holding a whip, with his eldest son John Day. Sam Day, junior, is seen in the foreground riding *Venison* and his brother William riding *Chapeau d'Espagne*, in Lord George Bentinck's colours. All are on the Danebury Downs with the hillfort in the background. The picture, painted in 1838, was considered the masterpiece of Abraham Cooper. (see frontispiece)

John and Anne's eldest son, John Barham Day (John Day the second), was born in 1793. A career as a jockey seems to have taken precedence over his education. Despite his tiny frame he became an outstanding jockey. He was regularly able to tip the scales at little over 7 stone (44.4 kg). He began his career riding at the minor tracks near his father's stables at Danebury. The fees for jockeys were very low, as was the standard of the racing.

Part of a caricature sculpture of John Barham Day (1793-1860) c.1835.
(by Guillemai)

Pussy with his trainer, John Barham Day.
(by John E. Ferneley)

In later years he took over the stables and was known as "Honest John" because he looked like a serious clergyman. He always carried a black cotton umbrella. He disliked smoking intensely, but not gambling, which it seems was a major passion of his. He professed to be greatly interested in the welfare and well being of his stable lads and jockeys. John B. Day's first great victory as a jockey came in 1826 for the Duke of Grafton, when he rode *Dervise* in the Two thousand Guineas, and *Problem* in the One Thousand Guineas, both of which he won over *Buckle*. For his efforts John received a gift of £20 and a lecture on the perils of suddenly acquired wealth. He was at one time jockey to King George IV. He lived with his family in Chattis Hill Cottage, which became known locally as Day's Cottage - a name which has stuck and lives on today in the nameplate on the cottage.

In 1832, with great support from Lord George Cavendish Bentinck, he transferred his training to Danebury next to the Stockbridge Racecourse, where the racing Lord and his friend Lord Sherborne put up a good deal of money to build the stables. Lord George's passion for the noble sport was legendary and he even appeared as a jockey himself on several occasions, before 1845. Under the noble Lords' patronage, the gallops and stables at Danebury were improved and many winners were trained. J.B. Day was probably the first full-time trainer and the first to apply professional methods.

Danebury Stables had over 100 employees in the house and stables all of which were kept under close scrutiny by the 'master', J.B. Day. The horses were never exercised on a Sunday, but the stable lads were required to attend church twice every Sunday, either at Nether Wallop or Stockbridge. Bible readings were held in the dining room of Danebury House every Sunday, at which any young apprentice not paying due attention would feel the crack of the master's whip across his shoulders. 'Old Sally' the cook took her seat by the hearth and the lads would sit at the table when J.B. entered on the stroke of the clock with due solemnity to read one of Blair's sermons.

The Days' strict regime extended also to the training of the horses and it was jokingly said they "...either suffered and survived – or it was the glue factory". They were often criticised for their extreme regime but the results achieved silenced their critics.

After only two years at Danebury, John Barham's first success in a classic race came when *Pussy* won The Oaks in 1834 with the 'master' himself in the saddle. He went on to train 16 classics winners, including three Derby winners. As a successful jockey, John Barham Day won the Oaks five times, but never himself rode a Derby winner.

J. B. Day and Lord George's association only lasted around four years after the hard-headed pair had a falling out over Bentinck's methods relating to the handling of *Crucifix*. This filly, which won the One Thousand and Two Thousand Guineas and The Oaks in 1836, broke down in training shortly after the Oaks. Lord George, knowing the horse had no chance in the Leger, laid heavy odds against her. It has also been suggested that the Days were found to be charging Lord George exorbitant fees in the training and care of his horses. It was more likely a combination of both arguments but whatever the cause, the result was that Lord Bentinck removed his horses overnight and lodged them with John Kent at Goodwood.

With the departure of Lord George's patronage the stables fell into the hands of the notorious 'Danebury Confederacy', an association of some four or five men headed by John Gully who were infamous for their double-dealing or 'fixing', as it might be known today. This notoriety was well founded as it was seen that horses, which were fully expected to romp home, did not finish; whilst others considered to be 'dead meat' achieved amazing victories, all to the consternation of the betting fraternity.

For all the troubles with the Danebury Confederacy, John Barham Day was considered eminent in his profession and was called upon in 1844 to give evidence before a Committee of the House of Commons on "gaming" and the desirability of horse racing, and its connection with the improvement of the horse. He was described by Lord William Lennox as "one of those in which the public placed entire confidence".

John Barham's and the Danebury Stables' first success in the Derby came in 1846 with *Pyrrhus the First* (ridden by Sam Day, John's brother), the same year as *Mendicant* won The Oaks and One Thousand Guineas. The one time prizefighter and champion of England, John Gully (later MP for Pontefract) owned *Pyrrhus*. The 1846 Derby was the first ever to be timed with *Pyrrhus* winning in 2 minutes 55 seconds, a slow time by modern standards.

The following year *Cossack* ridden by Sim Templeman won the Derby for the Danebury Stables; it was owned by John Gully's son-in-law, a Mr Pedley, who was a bookmaker. The stables' third Derby win was with *Andover*, a horse bred by William Etwall at Longstock Park. William was brother of the MP for Andover, Ralph Etwall. The winning horse's owner was once again John Gully, whose other horse *Hermit* acted as pacemaker for *Andover* throughout the race – the jockey was Alfred Day, the trainer's son. *Hermit* had earlier that season won the Two Thousand Guineas and did his job so well in the Derby that year that he came in to finish third.

The *Illustrated London News* of 3 June 1854 printed a drawing of the Derby winner, *Andover*, at Epsom and described the event in detail with the betting at 7 to 2 against *Andover*, 10 to 1 against *King Tom*, 20 to 1 each against the *Hermit* and *Early Bird*:

> After the usual preparatory canter, the horses returned to the paddock, and were soon called to the post by the starter. The 'coup d'oeil' at this moment was extremely picturesque: the thousands of spectators surging up against the rails – the vast masses on the hill-side – the multitude crowding

the enclosures and the Grand Stand – had their eyes immediately riveted, as it were, on one point – the starting place. Slowly, and in a compact form, the horses proceeded towards it from the paddock, the colours of the riders having a gorgeous effect in the broad sunshine. At the very first signal a beautiful start was affected. *Hospodar* immediately went into the front with *Marc Antony*, *Canute* and *Wild Huntsman* heading the ruck. On nearing the turn, *Wild Huntsman* ran up to *Hospodar,* and *Dervish* lay about sixth. *Marc Antony* and *Canute* then dropping off. At the road, both *Hospodar* and *Dervish* were beaten. *Hermit* now took the lead...

Andover waited to the half distance, when he went ahead, followed by *King Tom*, who made a very resolute effort, but was beaten easily by a length. Half a length between the second and third, and a neck between the third and fourth. *Dervish*, *Marsayas*, *New Warrior*, and *Wild Huntsman* were the next four. Value of the stakes, £5950.

The Danebury Confederacy

John Gully was a great friend of Harry Hill and after losing most of his money, he parted with his home Ackworth Park (near Pontefract) to him. Not satisfied with the legitimate receipts of their joint ownership of racehorses, they decided to increase their takings by devious schemes. One such involved the laying of bets on horses ("dead uns") that they knew would not run, or stood little chance if they did, by the stable boys on behalf of their employers. This practice angered the betting fraternity considerably and was "odious in the sight of every man of principle", wrote William Day. "As odious as the practice was it was not directly illegitimate, least not so until they became discontent with this practice and began laying on bets on their own account." They began using the stable boys and young jockeys for intelligence in their bid to pull the wool over the eyes of the bookies, but in such a way as to avoid detection.

On one occasion at Newmarket Races Harry Hill was fairly caught and shown up for his devious tactics when a Mr Rayner requested that he put down £500 on a particular horse and he agreed to do so. The next day after the horse had won the race, Hill was asked for the money but he could not produce any winnings. "I did not put it on" was the reply, "and I forgot to declare so before the race." Mr Rayner denounced Hill as a liar and a scoundrel, not tolerating such a lame excuse and suggesting if he and Gully treated all customers in the same way they would soon have none at all.

Harry Hill was a wealthy man having amassed a huge fortune on the turf with his nefarious dealings. Another of the confederacy was a Mr Pedley, a north countryman from Huddersfield, who also had a number of horses trained at Danebury, one of which was *Cossack*, which won the Derby in 1847. He married one of John Gully's daughters and in so doing became one of the Danebury racing Confederacy. One of his creditors was Mr Fred Swindell for £300 who took his prize in wines of rare vintages from his collection.

Findon Down Stables

　　John Barham Day formally dissociated himself from the Danebury Confederacy in 1845 when he moved to Michel Grove, Findon in East Sussex, to act as private trainer to the solicitor, money-lender and erstwhile confederacy member, Henry Padwick. He is described by the Findon historian Valerie Martin as ".. a typical habitually dour Victorian. He was rather calculating and his traditional training methods were those of over-working his charges and breaking their spirits. He was a countryman, but certainly no country gentleman. Horses had to learn the hard way with Old John Day who believed that harsh treatment was good for them."[19]

　　John B. Day was well known to be as hard on his horses as he was on their owners, galloping them uphill, often in rugs and blankets. His regime of sweats, drenching, purging, and even bleeding, favoured the tough horses but it did result in heavy casualties. Day believed in sending his horses to post very fit and with little room for improvement and it was well known that Danebury runners were unusually successful first time out. Both of his sons who took to training followed similar methods.[20]

Virago, 1851. Trained by J.B. Day, seen standing with Will Goater (kneeling). Ridden by Wells in J.B. Day's colours (black jacket, orange cap) although she was the property of Henry Padwick, hence the 'P' on the horse blanket that Will Goater is holding.
(painted by Tom Barrett of Stockbridge)

After John Barham Day left for Findon his son, John Day the third (1814-1882) took over the Danebury stables and in 1867 sent out 146 winners (a record, which was equalled but not broken until 1987). He employed two of the country's most successful jockeys, George Fordham and Tom Cannon. William Day (1823-1908) another of J.B. Day's sons left Danebury in 1849 to set up his own stables at Woodyates, in Dorset. He too became a successful trainer and writer on the art of training racehorses and, in his later years, of his reminiscences and tales of the racing characters he had met.

William Day, 1891

Sometime during 1854 the Findon stables' patron, Henry Padwick, had a disagreement over the Two Thousand Guineas race in which his horse, the favourite *St. Hubert*, was beaten by *Lord of the Isles* ridden by John's son William. The Day family were accused by Padwick of fixing the race and shortly after John B. Day departed the scene to be replaced by William Goater.

It was not uncommon in racing circles to set up a match-making race between two of the country's most highly prized horses, allowing private betting of considerable magnitude amongst the landed gentry. One such race was set up at Newmarket in 1858 for a prize of £3,000, when *Anton* was pitted against *Kent*; Alfred Day rode *Anton* on the day and won the race by a neck. But a previous match held in 1851 at York between *The Dutchman* and *Voltigeur* did not come in for the Danebury patrons and John Day, as they suffered a large stake loss when *Voltigeur* romped home. The practice of match-making races slowly died away until by the 1880s the number of races per year was in the single figures.

John Barham Day was twice married but little is known except that his first wife's family name was Goddard and they had twelve children, two of which rode professionally: Alfred and Samuel, who won the St Leger on *Mango*.

Under the Hammer

The Houghton Down Estate, on which the first John Day settled to begin the Day family's association with Stockbridge, came under the auctioneer's hammer on 15th July 1870 at the Grosvenor Hotel. Lord George Bentinck, as a part payment for John Day the first's move to Danebury to train his horses, originally purchased the estate from the Day family. The catalogue described it as "A valuable estate, known as the Houghton Down Estate, containing about 41a. rr. 17p. comprising Houghton Down Farm, Houghton Down House, an extensive Range of Racing Stables, Training Grounds and Paddocks." The bidding commenced at £10,000 and the lot was eventually sold for £14,000.

Many prominent men in Hampshire owned horses trained at Danebury, among them Lord Palmerston of Broadlands, Romsey who was not interested in seeing them run or ever backed them. He would however occasionally ride over to see them in training and he held John Barham Day in high regard. Other owners who placed their horses at Danebury included Sir Lewin Glyn who commenced his racing interests in 1828; Lord Sligo, who although little known on the English turf kept just one or two horses at a time at Danebury but had a larger stud in Ireland; and Lord Glenlyon, a Scottish noble who commenced his racing career in 1843 at Danebury with *Ben y Ghlo* and *Pharold*, both of which were winners. Mr Pryse-Pryse of Buscot Park, Aberystwyth was one of the earliest patrons of Danebury and he also had horses with John Day before the move from Houghton Down Farm.

Ralph Etwall, who was for many years the Liberal Member of Parliament for Andover was another gentleman with interests at Danebury from 1832 until around 1849. Another local owner was Sir John Barker Mill of Mottisfont Abbey, who rarely had success with his horses; his sporting pursuits also included cock fighting at two inns near to his home. It was his cousin who caused the closure of Stockbridge Racecourse in 1898.

CHAPTER FOUR

TOM CANNON, CHAMPION JOCKEY AND TRAINER

John Barham Day died at the home of his brother William, at Woodyates, Dorset in 1860. He was succeeded by his son, John Day the third, who became an even more successful trainer than his father. In 1867 he had 146 winners. Among his stable jockeys were George Fordham and then Tom Cannon, who joined the stables in 1860. Born in Eton, the son of a Windsor horse dealer, Tom was 14 when he joined the Day stables as an apprentice. He had previously received some training as a jockey at Newmarket and Marlborough and for a short period in early 1860 he worked at the stables of William Sextie, an artist and racehorse trainer.

The young Tom's skills in the saddle were noted and he was given his first mount that same year at a race meeting in Plymouth. Tom's horse was a filly named *Mavourneen* but he could hardly have had a more disastrous start for his horse stumbled and he was thrown from the saddle. He recovered however and the following day brought home his first winner, *My Uncle*. After that Tom Cannon went from strength to strength at Danebury. He began as second jockey to George Fordham and later became the stable's number one.

Tom Cannon c.1900

Tom, although a 'natural' jockey, had a bit of a weight problem from time to time and took strenuous measures in order to bring himself to weight and fitness on race days. One of his methods was to don several large woollen sweaters and run around Danebury Racecourse.

In 1860 the Danebury Stables and gallops covered some 2,340 acres, but there was only one well and so two large underground tanks were constructed to provide water for the horses. As time went by Tom Cannon became an invaluable trainer at the stables, taking on more and more duties with both horses and jockeys. In bad weather he exercised the horses in the shadow of Danebury Ring.

Tom married John Day's daughter Kate on 13th December 1865. Tom and Kate had a large family but Kate died aged only 48 and is buried in Nether Wallop churchyard. They had four sons, Tom, Mornington, Kempton and Charles all of whom became successful jockeys, and seven daughters. (One of the daughters, Margaret, married Ernie Piggott, the son of a Cheshire farmer and a trainer and dealer in horses. Margaret and Ernie produced three sons, Ernest, Charles and Keith, who all went on to be good jockeys. Keith Piggott married Iris Rickaby from another racing family and they had a son Lester (born 1935), who went on to become one of the greatest jockeys this country ever produced and certainly the premier jockey of the 1970s and 80s.)

Tom Cannon was a natural jockey riding some 1,544 winners and a worthy adversary to Fred Archer, whom Tom admired greatly. He won the Two Thousand Guineas four times, the Ten Thousand Guineas three times, the Oaks four times and the St. Leger once. He also won the Grand Prix de Paris five times and the French Derby twice in his racing career. It could be said that the Derby of 1882 was Tom Cannon's supreme moment when, riding for the trainer John Porter of Kingsclere, he rode *Shotover* to a three-quarters of a length win. In addition to riding for the Days, Tom also rode for the stable managed by his brother Joseph in Bedford Cottage Yard at Newmarket; there his mounts included Lord Lonsdale's *Pilgrimage* on which he won the One Thousand Guineas and Two Thousand Guineas in 1878.

The 1881 Census for Danebury records John Day aged 66 now widowed as head of the household and a trainer of racehorses with his son Leonard, aged 35 and also widowed, as the assistant trainer. There were four female domestic servants, six stablemen and 15 apprentice trainers. The same Census also records William Day (57) living in Shipton Bellinger with his wife Ellen Day (59), their widowed daughter Harriet Good (30) and their son James Day (22) an unmarried medical student. Harriet's children, Kathleen and George, also lived there as well as a live-in parlour maid. William was a well-known trainer and author of *The Racehorse in Training* in which he remarks, "… show me a better system and I shall be happy to adopt it." The system adopted for training the horses at Danebury was considered severe and often meant that the horses ran light.

Tom Cannon on Shotover when he won the Derby Stakes in 1882. Shotover was trained by John Porter at Kingsclere and was owned by the Duke of Westminster.

John Day had a keen interest in fox hunting and kept his own pack of hounds at Danebury, which eventually were taken over by Tom Cannon. Many of Day's clients at the stables were keen huntsmen including Lords Courtenay, Howard and Andover, Henry Chaplin M.P., Sir Claude de Crespigny and others. Very often their lordships' interest in racing developed as a direct result of hunting and the desire to pit their favourite steed against each other's.[21]

After John Day the third died in 1883, the racecourse and training grounds of Danebury passed to his son-in-law, Tom Cannon. Tom somehow combined his racing with managing the stables and racecourse. The Cannons lived at 'Garlogs', Nether Wallop and Tom's pride and joy, his flock of sheep, won many prizes. Tom retired from racing in 1891 to put all his efforts into the training establishment at Danebury and the nearby Chattis Hill Stables.

The 1891 Census shows the Danebury household as follows:

> Thomas Cannon, head, married, 44, Trainer & Jockey, Employer, born at Eton in Buckinghamshire.
> … Alice Cannon, Daughter, spinster, aged 24, born Winchester, Hampshire
> … Leticia Cannon, Daughter, spinster, aged 20, born Houghton, Hampshire
> … Thomas Cannon, Son, aged 19, Jockey, born Houghton, Hampshire
> … Louisa Cole, Servant, aged 40, Housekeeper, Dublin, Ireland
> … Minnie Short, Servant, aged 31, Housekeeper, Plymouth, Devon

Garlogs at Nether Wallop in 1905, once the home of Tom Cannon and his family.

John Day the third in later life.　　　　　　　*National Portrait Gallery, London*
(watercolour by John Flatman)

... Emma Hiscock, Servant, aged 30, Cook Domestic Servant, Lyndhurst, Hampshire

... Caroline Rivers, Servant, aged 21, Cook Domestic Servant, Poole, Dorset

... Edith Amos, Servant, aged 21, Housemaid Domestic Servant, Southampton, Hampshire

Tom married for a second time in 1893 to Jessie Catherine, daughter of the late Duncan Cameron of Fort William, Inverness and they had one son. By 1895 he was described in a directory as "Proprietor of The Grosvenor Family & Commercial Hotel and Posting House", with Robert Henry Russell as the manager. Tom was also described as a wine and spirit merchant & refreshment contractor.[22]

The Grosvenor Hotel still contains some memorabilia of the racing era, including the pokerwork carvings in the restaurant done during Tom Cannon's proprietorship. Tom was a shrewd businessman and in 1894 he had 29 winners, netting the stables some £9,863 in prize money alone. He had 83 horses in training from eight owners, including Leopold de Rothschild, a close friend and confidant of the Prince of Wales.

On 1st March 1895 the *Andover Advertiser* carried an article entitled 'Training Boys and Horses' in which Edward Skeates, an apprentice to Mr. T. Cannon of Danebury, was summoned for a breach of his apprenticeship contract:

> Service of the summons having been proved, Mr. Groom, agent for Mr. Cannon, produced the Indentures between defendant and Mr. Cannon, signed May 15th, 1893. Defendant served under the Indentures until January 27th last, when he left, and had not returned since. All the conditions, as far as the master was concerned, had been carried out. Defendant had been punished on the 27th Jan. for telling an untruth, and for neglect of duty. He was punished by Mr. Olding, the head man, with a whip. William Olding, the trainer for Mr. Cannon, said that on 27th Jan. he found that defendant had not finished grooming his horse properly. He said he had, and for this untruth witness then gave him three or four cuts with the whip.

> - In reply to the Bench, witness added that he often had to administer this kind of punishment to the lads to keep them in order. He had had occasion to punish defendant previously. Defendant did not give witness any notice of his Intention to leave, and he did not know he was gone until he returned later on to the stable and found defendant missing. - Defendant was ordered to return and carry on his duties, and to pay the costs, 5s.6d.

Chattis Hill House and Stables

Tom Cannon built the Chattis Hill stables, between the years 1897 and 1898, as an adjunct to the Danebury stables, accommodating around sixty horses, with training

Chattis Hill House, Stockbridge in 1905. Another home of the Cannon family.

Chattis Hill Stables in 1905.

grounds and paddocks covering almost 350 acres. They later came under the ownership of Mr Henry Seymour ("Atty") Persse who went on to build a racing legend of his very own. He bred and trained *The Tetrarch* (owned by Major MacCalmont) which foaled in 1911 and became one of the fastest two year olds ever known. Popular with the 'locals', the horse's colouring with white and grey splodges gained him the nicknames "Spotted Wonder" and "Soapsuds". He was never beaten but shortly before the Derby his leg was injured and he never ran again. There is a painting of *The Tetrarch* on the screen in front of St. Peter's Church in Stockbridge. Steve Donahue was perhaps "Atty" Persse's most famous jockey and he lived locally in Stockbridge.

In 1904 Tom Cannon built Chattis Hill House, which stood in well laid-out grounds only 200 yards from the training stables.

Chattis Hill's RAF History

During the First World War, in the summer of 1917, the area around Chattis Hill House was converted into a rough grass aerodrome for use by the Royal Flying Corps. They used the field until the end of 1919 when it was abandoned, together with buildings that were in the first phase of construction. The land was returned to agricultural use and the training of racehorses in 1920.

Just 20 years later, following the bombing of the two Supermarine works at Woolston and Itchen near Southampton on 26 September 1940, the government requisitioned Chattis Hill as a dispersal and production centre for Spitfire aircraft. The new airfield, heavily camouflaged, was to the west of the old WWI aerodrome and was operational by December 1940. The first aircraft was delivered in March 1941, having been built in sheds erected on Chattis Hill Racing Gallops. It closed as an airfield in 1945 but remained an aircraft assembly plant until 31 May 1948. The assembly sheds were then removed and the fields were once again returned to pasture and the site reverted to what it is best known for – the training of racehorses.

Cannon 'the Huntsman'

For many years Tom Cannon hunted the district with his own pack of harriers and at the close of the season moved on to hunting deer. In retirement he bought Springfields, a rather beautiful country house in London Road, Stockbridge and he adorned the gateposts with a pair of old military cannons; he died in residence in 1917. After it was sold the house was renamed Cannon Lodge but the two cannons on the gateposts have long since disappeared and the only permanent memorials to Tom's life are the plaque in the Grosvenor Hotel and his tomb in the churchyard at the foot of Somborne Hill.

In 1884 Tom asked his friend and one time employer, William Sextie, who by then had built up quite a reputation as a painter and exhibited at the Royal Academy, to paint a portrait of him with two of his sons and his horses exercising on the Stockbridge Racecourse. The picture became known as 'Recollection of Stockbridge'. It was highly prized and for many years hung in Tom Cannon's quarters at the Grosvenor Hotel in Stockbridge. The whereabouts of this painting are now unknown as it disappeared after his death in 1917.

Before Tom died the Danebury estate had been divided with Danebury House passing into the ownership of W.T. Moore, a successful jockey and trainer whose horses had many successes in the Grand National, including *Manifesto*, which won twice, *Why Not* and *The Soarer*. (The small unmade lane leading off from The Avenue in Andover toward the Rank Hovis Mill in Mylen Road was named Whynot Lane in celebration of the Grand National win.) By 1912 Danebury had passed into the ownership of Mr F.E. Withington, another of this country's great trainers.

The last resting place of Tom Cannon and his wife, Jessie, in Stockbridge Cemetery

Today the Danebury House estate has a rather different use for now grape vines grow where once the racehorses trained on the gallops. The Danebury vineyard when originally planted in 1988 covered an area of three acres. The current owner, Mr Ernst Piëch, purchased Danebury Vineyard in 1993 and decided to make both a sparkling and a still wine. The wines were named after two horses trained at Danebury who went on to win the Derby in the 1840s. The sparkling wine is known as *Cossack* and the still wine *Pyrrhus*. In 2001 the tasting rooms and gardens were renovated and offered a range of menus to compliment the fine wines. The Danebury Vineyards still continue the racing legacy by sponsoring an important race at Salisbury Racecourse "The Danebury Vineyards Handicap".

The original Danebury Stables and part of the gallops are still used to train racehorses and the current owners, Danebury Racing Stables Ltd., under their trainer, Ken Cunningham-Brown, have had many successes throughout the racing world. Ken is also the Managing Director of Andover Town Football Club, and Unicheq Ltd.

Aerial view of the old racecourse on Danebury Downs, 2002

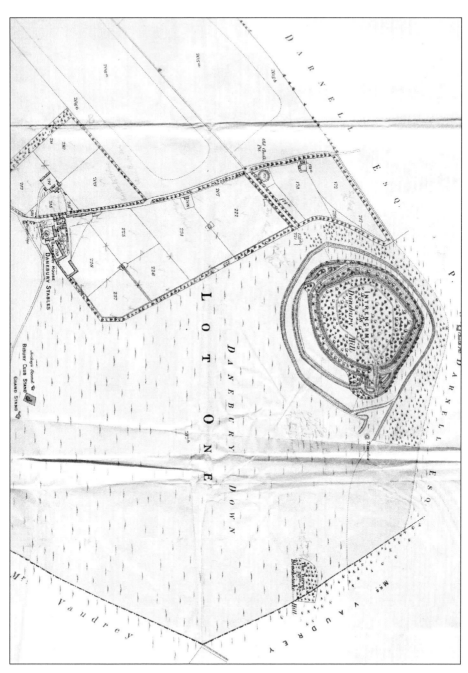

Part of the map issued with the Danebury sale particulars, 1907.

47

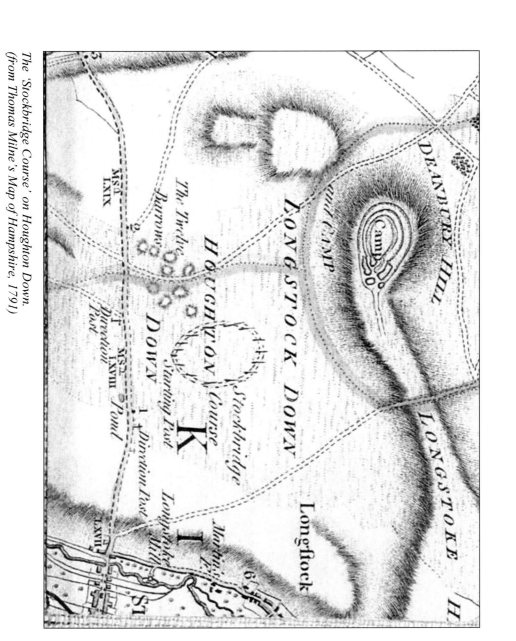

The 'Stockbridge Course' on Houghton Down.
(from Thomas Milne's Map of Hampshire, 1791)

John Barham Day with his sons John and William, 1841.
(painted by Harry Hall)

Tom Cannon.
(cartoon by Spy in Vanity Fair, 1885)

The Stockbridge Race 'Cup'.
(made by C.F. Hancock, parcel-gilt, 1870-1)
        The Metropolitan Museum of Art, Gift of Margaret A. Darrin, 1990 (1990.153)
        Photograph © 1990 The Metropolitan Museum of Art

A NOTE ON LORD GEORGE BENTINCK

Lord William George Henry Cavendish Bentinck (1802-1848) was the son of William Henry Cavendish-Scott-Bentinck, the 4th Duke of Portland. Initially he began a military career, but after a dispute with his superior officer he changed direction, becoming private secretary to his uncle, George Canning, when Canning was Foreign Secretary and leader of the House of Commons. Lord George later entered politics himself and was M.P. for Lynn from 1828 until his death.

Starting out as a Whig (the fore-runners of the Liberals), he later joined the Conservative opposition. He was offered and refused government office on two occasions. He took a more public line in 1845 when he became an active Protectionist, bringing him into an alliance with Disraeli, who advised him on matters of party tactics. By 1846, Lord George was a central figure in organising the Protectionists as a third political party, and he reluctantly came forward to lead the party. He was an influential leader but after differences with the party on religious matters in 1847 he announced his resignation, but remained a prominent upholder of the cause.

Lord William George Bentinck.
(an engraving after Sir Thomas Lawrence, PRA)

Politics to one side, the main passion in Lord George Bentinck's life was for the turf. Gambling was in his blood and when he was only 26 he is said to have lost around £26,000 in debts at Doncaster. His father did his utmost to deter his son from gambling to the extent of giving him an estate in Argyle in an attempt to divert his thoughts, but to no avail.

In 1832 Lord George Bentinck transferred his horses to the Day family stables and with his patronage John Barham Day moved from Houghton Down to Danebury next to the Stockbridge Racecourse, where many winners were trained. Under the patronage of Lord George and his friend Lord Sherborne, the stables flourished and they ran a successful stud with John Day as trainer. In 1844 Bentinck had 40 horses running in public, and around 100 in total. In order to see his string of horses in training, Lord George would travel down from London in his large yellow carriage the night before the race meeting to stay at the Star & Garter Hotel in Andover and get up early the next morning to be at the stables at Danebury before 5am. He would then ride his grey mare onto the downs to watch the horses exercise.

He was a heavy, though seemingly successful, gambler and experienced considerable success with his horses. He also worked hard to improve horseracing practices. In 1840 his filly, *Crucifix*, won the One Thousand Guineas, The Oaks and St Leger. He often resorted to pseudonyms in order to hide his gambling and vast racing interests and raced his horses in the names of Mr. John Bowe, a publican, Mr. King, the Duke of Richmond and John Day.

A more interesting winner was *Elis* at the St Leger in 1836. Lord George was dissatisfied with the odds against the horse, a mere five to one, and refused to send the horse to Doncaster until better odds were forthcoming. When it was considered that there was insufficient time to get the horse from Danebury to Doncaster in time the odds against the horse winning rose to ten thousand to one and the bet was laid. Lord George borrowed a large van, constructed for the purpose of carrying show cattle, from Lord Chesterfield and in this van pulled by four post-horses, *Elis* was safely conveyed to the racecourse, arriving fresh and surprising the bookmakers who had assumed that Lord George would have arranged that the horse would have come on foot, which was the practice until then.

After this trial run a much more commodious and purpose built horsebox was made in Nether Wallop and in 1837 *Crucifix* and *Sal-volatile* were driven in it to Newmarket, where *Crucifix* after winning the July Handicap, ran a dead heat for the Chesterfield Stakes. William Day and W. Goater attended on the day.

Lord George never married. He died in 1848 at the age of 46 from a heart attack whilst out walking near Welbeck Abbey.

The University of Nottingham has a large collection of the letters and papers of Lord George Bentinck in the Portland Collection. Bentinck discusses with his racing advisor, John Kent, the horses he is preparing for race in the years 1843-45, as well as the conspiracy theory he holds with regard to John Barham Day and the way he exercises the horses. There is also an exercise book with a report in it of events pertaining to the 1840 Derby and an altercation between John Gully and Mr Hargreave in 1845.

RACECARDS 1851-1898

The following represents the total of the racecards I have been able to find relating to Stockbridge Racecourse. Some are fragmentary made up from contemporary newspaper reports. Those that have access to Ruff's Guides may be able to add to the database.

Stockbridge Racecourse 1851
Thursday 20th June, 1851
The Bibury Club Meeting

Handicap of £40, with £10 for the second T.Y.C.		First Stockbridge Triennial Stakes of 10 sovs each for 4-y-o (Two miles and a half)		Second Triennial Stakes of 10 sovs each for 3-y-o (One mile and a half)		Third Triennial Stakes of 10 sovs each, for 2-y-o T.Y.C.	
Lord Clifden's Sagacity, aged, 11st 2lb (Mr. P. Williams)	1	Mr Grenville's Cariboo (3lb allowed, 5lb extra) Flatman	1	Mr J Powney's Lamartine (A. Day)	1	Col. Peel's Kingston, 8st 7lb (Fatman)	1
Mr. Herbert's c by Sir Hercules out of Adela, 3 yrs, 9st 3lb (Mr. Henry)	2	Lord Enfield's The Beefhunter (A. Day)	2	Mr E. R. Clarke's Glenhawk (Dockersey)	2	Mr. Dorrien's br c Chief Baron Nicholson 8st 7lb (Dockeray)	2
Mr. Waller nd New Forest Deer, aged, 11st 2lb (Mr Bevill)	3			Lord Exeter's Phiegethon (Norman)	3	5 to 4 on Kingston 9 to 4 agst Joe Miller	
				Duke of Richmond's Hurry Scurry (Kitchener)	4	A dead heat between Kingston and Chief Baron Nicholson;	
				Mr R. Etwall's Iracundus (Rogers)	5	Joe Miller a bad third.	

Run in 1min. 29 secs.

Second heat: 6 to 5 on Chief Baron Nicholson. AQ splendid race ended in another dead heat. Alfred Day rode Chief Baron Nicholson in this heat. The stakes were divided.

**Stockbridge Plate of
50 sovs for all ages
T.Y.C.**

was won in three
heats Mr. Stottard's
Woodsprite, 4yr,
(£25)   **1**
Mr. Hughe's f by
Cowl out of
Celandine, 3 yrs
(£100),   **2**
Mr Payne's
Guardsman, 3 yrs   **3**
several others.

Thursday 25th June, 1886
Stockbridge Meeting

The Second Year of the Twenty-Seventh Biennial Stakes of 10 sovs each [for 3-y-o] (A mile and a half)

Mr Mantou's Gay Hermit, by Hermit-Doll Tearsheet, 9st F. Archer   **1**
Mr J.A. James's Astrachan, 9st W. Lashmar   **2**
Lord Zetland's Jewel Song, 9st 9lb J. Watts   **3**

9 to 5 on Gay Hermit, 5 to 2 agst Jewel Song, 100 to 30 agst Astrachan

Won length,
Neck second and third.

Wallop Plate (selling H'cap) of 100 guineas (New mile)

Mr T. Cannon's Iceburg, by Dutch Skater-Hesperia, 4y 11st Hon G. Lambton   **1**
Mr Mantou's Stourwood, 3y 11st Mr Bevill   **2**
Mr Sadler's Nightingale, 4y 11st Mr Barclay   **3**
Mr Partridge's Attadale, 4y 11st 7lb Mr E.M. Owen   **0**
Mr Goodman's Bertie II, aged 10st 7lb Mr C. Beard   **0**

7 to 4 agst Stourwood, 2 to 1 agst Iceburg 9 to 2 agst Nightingale, 5 to 1 agst Bertie II

Won 3 lengths,
A bad third

Winner not sold.

The Alington Plate (selling H'cap)] of 100 sovs. Bush in (5f)

Mr T.E. Waller's Princess Maud, by Thurie-Grand Duchess, 3y 7st 9lb (car. 7st 10lb) P. Barrett   **1**
Mr R. Ten Brocck's Fleta, 5y 9st T. Cannon   **2**
Mr D. Henty's Clarewood, 6y 9st 11lb J. Watts   **3**
M T. Leuden's Gwendraeth, 4y 8st 4lb W. Lasmar   **0**
Mr R. Tompkins's Mariner, 3y 8st 4lb Sherratt   **0**
Mr F.R. Hunt's Alda, 3y 7st 7lb F. Barrettt   **0**

6 to 4 agst Princess Maud, 4 to 1 each agst Fleta and Alda, 5 to 1 agst Gwenraeth, 100 to 8 each agst Clarewood and Mariner

Won by a head; Second and third a head.

Winner sold to Mr Coles for 200gns

The Hurstbourne Stakes of 50 sovs. [for 2-y-o] Bush in (5f)

Mr T Jenning, jun's Mamia, by Speculuna-Mayfly, 8st 11lb T. Cannon   **1**
Mr Abington's Jack o'Lantern, 9st J. Watts   **2**
General O. William's Vatican, 8st 11lb (car. 9st) F. Archer   **3**

6 to 1 on Jack o'Lantern, 10 to 1 agst Mamia, 100 to 30 Napoleon 5 to 1 Mephisto.

Won three parts of length,
A bad third.

53

The Hunters' Plate of 100 guineas (Two miles)

Mr F. Garnham's Amy, by Remourse-Whitlock, 4y 11st 2lb (£50) Mr Bevill	**1**
Captain Child's King's County, aged 12st 2lb Hon.G. Lambton	**2**
Mr S. Woodland's Miss Annie, aged 12st 2lb (£50) Mr E.M. Owen	**3**
Mr H.T. Barclay's Canute, 6y 12st 12lb (£50) owner	
Mr A Yates's Bayonet, aged 12st 2lb Capt. Morris	**0**
Baron C. de Tuyll's Beckhampton, aged 12st 2lb (£50) Mr H. Owen	**0**
Sir, C.C. de Creapigny's Imogene, 5y 11st 2lb (£50) owner	**0**
Mr H. Drummond's Manfred, 4y 11st 2lb (£50) Capt. E, R. Owen	

2 to 1 agst Amy,
5 to 2 agst Beckhampton,
4 to 1 agst King's County,
100 to 12 agst Manfred,
12 to 1 each agst others.

Won by 6 lengths,
A bad third.

Winner bought for 210 gns

An All-Aged Plate of 105 sovs (5f)

Mr Ten-Broeck's Fleta, by Wenlock-Indecision, 6y 9st 4lb F. Archer	**1**
Mr Chandler's Ronald, 9st 7lb J. Watts	**2**
Captain Child's Ludlow, 2y 7st (car. 7st 1lb) F. Rickaby	**3**
Mr T. Cannon's Baritone, 2y 7st W. Robinson	**0**
Mr Coombe's c. by Blair Athol-Westena, 3y 8st 12lb G. Barrett	**0**
Lord Rosebery's Fish Smart, 2y 7st T Loates	**0**

13 to 8 agst Fish Smart,
9 to 4 agst Fleta,
6 to 4 agst Ronald,
7 to 1 agst Ludlow
100 to 8 agst Baritone

Won by a head,
A bad third.

Winner bought for 20 gns

Her Majesty's Plate of 300 sovs (2 miles)

Mr D. Baird's Bird of Freedom, by Thuringian Prince-Vitula, 4y 9st. F. Archer	**1**
Captain Fisher's Dalesman, 6y 9st 4lb Giles	**2**
Mr Sadler's Vain Hope, 3y 7st 8lb F. Rickaby	**3**
Mr Barclay's Criterion, 5y 9st 4lb G. Barrett	**0**
Mr Yates's Cutlet, 6y 8st 4lb Guy	**0**
Lord Zetland's War Path, 4y 9st J. Watts	**0**

5 to 4 on Bird of Freedom,
100 to 30 agst War Path,
8 to 2 agst Criterion,
20 to 1 each agst Vain Hope and Dalesman,
100 to 1 agst Cutlet.

Won by half a length,
A bad third.

Troy Stakes of 50 sovs For 2-y-o Bush in (5f)

Mr Abington's Alarm (late Cockcrow), by Peter-Maid of Perth, 8st 9lb J. Watts	**1**
Mr Manton's Mezzotint, 8st 9lb T. Cannon	**2**

5 to 4 on Alarm

Won by a neck

Stockbridge Racecourse 1889
Tuesday 2nd July, 1889
The Bibury Club Meeting (Good Going)

Match of £58, both 2-y-o; Bush in (5f)

450 Mrs Eyre's Try
Again
8-11 w.o.

Fourth Zetland Stakes (biennial (New mile)

532 Duke of Westminster's Ormuz 8-12 G Barrett	**1**
549 Pinxon 8-12 J Watts	**2**

3 to 1 on Ormuz

Won neck.

Scurry Welter (selling handicap of £125 (1m)

475 Mr R Moncreiffe's Martinet 6y 11-9 Owner	**1**
556 Yum Yum 2y 11-7 Mr Coventry	**2**
299 Anacreon 3y 11-7 Mr H Owen	**3**
328 The Skipper 3y 11-9 Mr A L Popham	**0**
447 Æolides 4y 11-10 Mr G Lamdon	**0**
475 La Reyne 3y 11-5 Mr H T Barclay	**0**

8 to 1 each agst
Martinet,
Yum Yum and
Æolides
5 to 1 The Skipper,
6 to 1 Anacreon and
La Reyne

Won three parts
length;
Bad third – winner not
sold.

Private Sweepstakes of £400, for 2-y-o. Bush in (5f)

513 Mr N Fenwick's Pluie d'Or 8-9 F Barrett	**1**
(519) Arcadia 8-9 G Barrett	**2**
(337) Imogene 9-0 Rickaby	**3**

6 to 4 agst each
Arcadia,
Imogene
7 to 1 Pluie d'Or

Won by short head;
Neck second and
third.

Champagne Stakes of £325 for 2-y-o Bush in (5f)

(401) Lord Zetland's
Margarine 8-12
J Watts   1
467 Lottie Smith 8-9
Warne   2
Merrie Monk 8-12
F Barrett   3
Chippenham 8-12
T Cannon jun   0
Bauble 8-12
Bickaby   0
412 C by Sterling-
Kathleen 8-12
G Barrett   0
Pertinax 8-12
Bradbury   0
506 Red Thorn 8-9
M
Cannon   0

Evens on Perseat,
3 to 1 agst Kilkerran,
5 Ebbing Tide,
10 Falster,
20 each Theale,
Silchester.

Won a head;
three quarters of a
length.

Houghton Selling Welter Plate of £100 (1m)

549 Skill 6y 12-4
Mr W H Moore   1
551 Moon 3y 10-10
Mr A Coventry   2
484* McCrankie
5y 12-4
Mr Lushington   3
496* Lal Lal 3y 10-7
Mr Grenfell   4
490 Acrefield 4y 12-0
Mr Barclay   5
557 St. Jude 6y 12-1
Mr Schwabe   –

6 to 5 on Margarine,
4 to 1 agnst, Merrie
Monk,
8 to 1 Lottie Smith
20 to 1 others..

Won by half a length;
half length second and
third.

Winner sold to
Mr F R Hunt 200gns.

Hampshire Stakes of £493, 3-y-o (1m)

410 Dynamo 8-12
Rickaby   1
549 Aureus 8-12
Toon   2
524 Faversham 8-12
G Chaloner   3
517 Brechin 8-5
Bradford   4
Dromeus 8-5
K Cannon   5
525 Conroy 9-5
M Cannon   –

15 to 8 on Conroy,
4 to 1 agst Aureus,
100 to 9 Brechin,
100 to 8 Faversham,
20 others.

Won a neck,
a head.

Bibury Stakes [Handicap] of £190 (1m 4f)

431 Mr J Davis's
White Flag 4y 11-12
Mr W H Moore   1
(146) Holly 5y 12-6
Mr H T Barclay   2
416 Balderdash
4y 12-0 G Lambton   3
142 Sanctury 6y 11-3
Mr E W Baird   0
438 Dhuleep Singh 3y
10-10
Mr A Coventry   0
473 Treasure 3y 10-3
Mr A L Popham   0

Evens on Holly,
4 to 1 agnst, Dhuleep
Singh,
6 to 1 White Flag
8 to 1 each Balderdash
and Sanctury
10 to 1 Treasure

Won three parts
length;
Bad third.

Plate of £100

(5f)

415 Mr O H Jones's
Dulce Domum 2y 6-6
Penton **1**
535 Mountain
Warbler 3y 8-0
G Barrett **2**
534 Rubric 2y 6-6
Brown **3**
Rosemarine 3y 8-9
T.
Cannon jun. **0**

13 to 8 on Dulce
Domum
9 to 2 agst Mountain
Warbler
6 to 1 Rubric

Won half length
Two lengths second
and third

Winner not sold.

**Match of £100, both
2-y-o
Bush in (5f)**

Mr T S Starkey's Eric
8-7 G Barrett **1**
Jumps 8-10 T
Cannon, jun **2**

2 to 1 on Eric.

Won length and a half

**Bibury Club Home-
bred Foal Stakes of
£605 (T.Y.C.)**

(508) Duke of
Portland's
Semolina 8-11 F
Barrett **1**
Albertine 8-1
J Watts **2**
501 Baracole 8-11
W Waroe **3**
431 Petrel 8-11
Rickaby **0**

9 to 2 on Semolina,
6 to 1 agst Albertine,
100 to 8 Baracole,

Won length and a half,
Three lengths second
and third.

**Match of £100, both
2-y-o
Bush in (5f)**

Mr W Lowe's
Mystery 8-10
G Barrett **1**
Daenae 8-11
J Watts **2**

5 to 1 on Mystery.

Won by half length

Thirty-first Biennial Stakes of £340 for 2-y-o (T.Y.C.)

Mr W. Goater's Spell
8-8 F Barrett   **1**
Union Jack 9-0
G Barrett   **2**
Bell Rock 9-0 T
Cannon jun   **3**
294 Bright Eyes 8-8
Bradbury   **0**
Gunter 8-11
M Cannon   **0**
470 Bonnie Glen 8-11
Warne   **0**
508 C by Lancastrian,
dam by Adventurer-
Wildflower 9-0
Rickaby   **0**

5 to 2 against Spell,
4 to 1 Bonnie Glen,
5 to 1 each Bell Rock
and Union Jack,
6 to 1 Lancastrian
colt,
10 to 1 others

Won two lengths,
Head second and
third.

Wednesday 3rd July, 1889
Stockbridge Meeting (Going Good)

Fifth Zetland Stakes (a biennial sweepstakes) of £225 (5f)

511 Prince Soltykoff's Keythorpe 8-12 M Cannon **1**
Ornament 8-9 G Barrett **2**

100 to 15 on Keythorpe,

Won length and a half,

Johnstone Plate (H'cap) of £100 (T.Y.C.)

437 Mr R Tomkins Minstrel Boy 6y 6-12 Allsop **1**
466 Molly Lepel 6y 6-9 Peak **2**
470 Coolshannagh 3y 6-4 Penton **3**
(451) Tartarus 3y 7-5 Anthony **4**
476 Maiden Belle 4y 8-3 F Barrett **5**
Primrose Day 4y 6-6 Dibben **6**
251 Nora 5y 8-13 J Watts **0**
431 Peck o' Pepper 4y 7-13 Blake **–**
411 Bob Sawyer 4y 7-13 Liddiard **–**
472 Camberwell Beauty 3y 6-12 Bradbury **–**
451 Miss Jack 4y 6-3 Brown **–**
Fire 4y 6-10 Richardson **–**

75 to 20 against Maiden Belle,
9 to 2 Minstrel Boy
6 to 1 Molly Lepel,
100 to 15 Tartarus,
8 to 1 Bob Sawyer,
10 to 1 Nora.
100 to 8 Primrose Day
100 to 7 Miss Jack,
100 to 6 Peck o' Pepper,
20 to 1 each Coolhannagh and Camberwell Beauty
50 to 1 Fire Damp

Won a neck,
Three-parts length second and third.

Danebury Plate [for 2-y-o] of £100 Bush in (5f)

254 Mr C Archer's Saucy Nell 8-9 T Loates **1**
451 Southern Queen 8-9 T Cannon jun. **2**
(543) Dulce Domum 8-9 Warne **3**
(541) F by Standard-Bryony 8-9 W. Goater **0**
544 Danaä 8-9 F Barrett **0**

5 to 4 agst Saucy Nell,
9 to 4 Dulce Dumum,
100 to 15 Southern Queen,
100 to 8 each Bryony filly and Danae

Won length and a half;
Second and third three lengths.

Winner sold to Mr Sneyd for 260gns

Stockbridge Cup of £300. (T.Y.C.)

554 Lord Hastings' St Patrick 3y 8-5 F. Barrett **1**
(513) Mr W. Lowe's Napoleon 3y 8-10 G. Barrett **2**
(539) Lord Penrbyns' Noble Chieftain 4y 9-6 Weidon **3**
513 Mephisto 6y 9-4 M. Cannon **0**

13 to 8 agst Noble Chieftain,
9 to 4 St. Patrick,
100 to 30 Napoleon
5 to 1 Mephisto.

Won half length,
Neck second and third.

Andover Stakes (H'cap) of £185 (Old mile)

542 Lord Zetland's
Pinzon 3y 11
Mr A Coventry   1
543 Balderdash
4y 12-2
Mr W. H. Moore   2
466 Lown a 11-10
Mr G. Lampton   3
318 Flumen 3y 10-5
Capt. Lee Barber   4
548 Treasure 3y 9-9
Mr Popham   –
(512) Martinet 6y 11
Mr Moncrieff   –
394 Earl of Shifnal
4y 10-7
Mr H. Owen   –
315 Spite 3y 10-1
Capt. Orr-Ewing   –

6 to 4 agst Lown,
100 to 30 Pinzon,
5 to 1 Flumen,
100 to 12 Balderdash,
10 to 1 Martinet.

Won by length,
Four lengths second
and
third.

Mottisfont Plate of £356 for 2-y-o Bush in (5f)

Mr H. S. Leon's
Swallowtail 7-13
{£200}
M. Cannon   1
520 First Fruit 8-9
Warne   2
543 C by Sterling-
Kathleen 8-2
G. Barrett   3
257 F by Foxhall-
Winter Queen 7-13
F. Peake   4
Lammas Day 8-2
W. Blake   0
299 Horoscope 8-9
T Cannon   0
Sweet Pea 8-19
F. Brown   0

11 to 8 agst
Swallowtail,
100 to 90 First Fruit,
100 to 12 Kathleen
colt, 20 to 1 others.

Won three lengths'
Same second and
third.

Winner sold to Mr
Sneyd for 1.020
guineas.

Beaufort H'cap Plate of £191 (1m 2f)

507 Mr W. Blake's
Exmoor 6y 9-4
O J. Watts   1
(543) White Flag 4y
7-8 T. Loates   2
543 Holly 5y 7-13
Liddiard   3
(505) True Blue II 6y
9-1 T. Cannon, jun. 4
430 Papyrus 4y 7-7
Peake   5
Theodolite 4y 7-5
Penton   0
249 Barmecide 3y 7-1
Allsopp   0
447 Marione 4y 7-1
Bradbury   0
515 Meadow Brown
3y 6-8 Dibben   0

3 to 1 agst Exmoor,
7 to 2 Holly,
6 to 1 Meadow
Brown,
100 to 15 True Blue
II,
7 to 1 Papyrus,
8 to 1 Marioni,
10 to 1 each White
Flag and Barmecide.

Won by a head,
Bad third.

Stockbridge Foal Stakes of £530 Bush in (5f)

(407) Mr C. W. Lee's
Prince of Tyre 8-13
Robinson   1
541 Fontainbleau 8-11
J. Watts   2
St. Andrew 8-11
G. Barrett   3

7 to 4 on Prince of
Tyre,
15 to 8 agst
Fontainbleau,
20 to 1 St. Andrew.

Won four lengths
Bad third.

60

Thursday 4th July, 1889
Stockbridge Meeting

Troy Stakes of £225 for 2-y-o Bush in (5f)

543 Mr Rowe's Lottie Smith 8-10 J Watts **1**
Hildago 9 G Barrett **2**

10 to 1 on Lottie Smith,

Won length.

Hunters Plate of £102 (2m on the flat)

109 Capt. Homfray's Mon Roi a 12-2 (£50) Lord Cholmondeley **1**
394 Will o' the Wisp 6y 12-2 Mr H. Owen **2**
(480) Le Expedicion a 12-2 Mr Popham **3**
51 Mounthrothe 6y 12-2 Mr Dudley Leigh **0**
480 Arthur 5y 11-2 0 Capt. Lee Barber **0**

6 to 4 agst Will o' the Wisp,
2 to 1 Nora Mon Roi
4 to 1 Athur
10 to 1 Others

Won 6 lengths
Bad third.

Winner bought in 230 guineas.

Allington Plate [selling handicap] of £100 Bush in (5f)

543 Mr H Yates's Mountain Warbler 3y G Barrett **1**
446 Jolly Tar (h-h) T Cannon jun. **2**
535 Lausanne 3y 7-10 Warne **0**
Cambric 4y 9 Robinson **0**
449 Montgomerie 3y 7-7 F Bradbury **0**

11 to 8 agst Mountain Warbler,
9 to 4 Jolly Tar,
11 to 2 Lausanne,
10 to 1 Montgomerie

Won head;
Bad third

Winner not sold.

Hurstbourne Stakes of £1,150 for 2-y-o. (5f)

(515) Mr H Millner's Riviera 8-11 T. Loates **1**
(545) Prince Soltykoff's Keythorpe 8-11 M. Cannon **2**
(539) Duke of Westminster's Blue-Green 9 G. Barrett **3**
503 Master Jack 9 J. Watts **0**

2 to 1 on Riviera,
75 to 20 agst Master Jack,
6 to 1 Keythorpe,
20 to 1 Blue-Green

Won length,
head second and third,
half-length third and fourth.

Wallop Plate [Selling H'cap] of £102 (1m)

385 Mr J. Davis's Cape
Race 3y 10-12 Mr
W.H. Moore   1
434 Sharper 4y 12 Mr
G Lambton   2
546 Treasure
3y 11-12
Mr Popham   3
543 Dhuleep Singh
3y 11
Mr Coventry -   0
542 La Reyne 3y 10-5
Mr Montcreiffe -   0

6 to 4 agst Dhuleep
Singh,
3 to 1 Sharper,
9 to 2 Treasure,
7 to 1 La Reyne.

Won easily by two
lengths;
a neck.

All-aged Plate [Selling] of £100 (5f)

546 Mr T. Cannon's
Southern Queen
2y 6-6 Brown   1
415 Escrick 2y 7
T Lownes   0

100 to 30 on Southern
Queen.

Won by six lengths.

Winner sold to Mr A
Yates for 50 gns.

Stockbridge Post Sweepstakes of £400 for 2-y-o (T.Y.C.)

544 D. of Portland's
Semolina 8-10
F. Barrett
                  w.

Second Year of the Thirteenth Biennial Stakes of £270 for 3-y-o (1½ miles)

384 Capt. L.H.
Jones's Theophilus
8-11
G. Barrett   1
                  w.

Stockbridge Racecourse 1896
Wednesday 7th July, 1896
The Bibury Club Meeting (Capital Going)

Bibury Club Junior Home Bred Stakes of £225 10s (5f)

Crest 9-2 J Watts	1
Baron Lumley 9-0 Allsopp	2
Kilgrain 9-5 Rickaby	3
558 Alberton 8-4 Bradford	4
523 Billion 9-0 M Cannon	–

11 to 8 on Baron
Lumley,
6 to 1 each and Crest,
Billion,
10 each Alberton,
Kilgrain.

Won by a short head,
six lengths.

Selling N.H. Flat Race of £97 (2m)

95* Baccarat 6y 12-7 Mr Cresswell	1
202* Unionist a 12-7 Mr Moore	2
105 Ltttle Boy Blue a12-7 Mr Coventry	3
99 Day Star a 12-7 Mr Barclay	4
455 Clansman II 6y 12-7 Mr Lawson	–
40 Piedra 5y 12-3 Mr Playne	–
364* War Qeen 4y 11-7 Mr Grenfell	–

13 to 8 agst Unionist,
9 to 4 Baccarat,
5 Little Boy Blue,
8 War Queen,
16 others.

Won easily by three
lengths;
six lengths.

Winner sold to Mr A
H Hudson 300gns.

Fullerton Handicap of £195 (6f)

557 Burgonet 3y 8-4 Madden	1
556 Castle Or 3y 7-10 Grimshaw	2
493 Lady Charity 3y 7-1 Toon	3
502 Honorious 5y 8-0 Allsopp	4
Lady Flippant 3y 7-8 Barlow	5
459 Attainment 3y 8-1 M Cannon	6
208 Nagpore 3y 7-5 S Loates	–
Melophoria 3y 7-2 K Cannon	–

9 to 4 agst
Attainment,
9 to 2 Castle Or,
11 to 2 Lady Charity,
13 to 2 Burgonet,
7 Honorious,
8 Nagpore,
25 to 2 Melophoria,
33 to 1 Lady
Flippant.

Won four lengths;
three parts of a length.

Bibury Stakes [Handicap] of £251 (1m 4f)

514 Anlaf 4y 11-5 Mr C Grenfell	1
513 Irish Wake 6y 12-8 Mr Coventry	2
478 Paddy a 12-7 Mr G Thursby	3
551 Vicar II 4y 11-0 Mr Lushington	4
518 Oregon a 11-9 Mr R Ward	5
343 Omar 4y 11-2 Mr Lawson	6
560 Meilekh 4y 11-6 Capt Bewicke	–
525 Carton Pierre 3y 10-7 Mr Milne	–

2 to 1 agst Vicar II,
4 Meilekh,
9 to 2 Anlaf,
8 each Paddy Carton
Pierre,
10 Irish Wake.

Won by a length and a
half; bad third.

Champagne Stakes of £325 for 2-y-o (5f)		Houghton Selling Welter Plate of £100 (1m)		Hampshire Stakes of £493, 3-y-o (1m)	
461* Kilkerran 9-1 J Watts	1	549 Skill 6y 12-4 Mr W H Moore	1	410 Dynamo 8-12 Rickaby	1
471* Perseat 8-12 S Loates	2	551 Moon 3y 10-10 Mr A Coventry	2	549 Aureus 8-12 Toon	2
451 Theale 8-9 K Cannon	3	484* McCrankie 5y 12-4 Mr Lushington	3	524 Faversham 8-12 G Chaloner	3
288 Falster 8-12 Allsopp	4	496* Lal Lal 3y 10-7 Mr Grenfell	4	517 Brechin 8-5 Bradford	4
357 Silchester 8-12 Rickaby	–	490 Acrefield 4y 12-0 Mr Barclay	5	Dromeus 8-5 K Cannon	5
474 Ebbing Tide 8-9 M Cannon	–	557 St. Jude 6y 12-1 Mr Schwabe	–	525 Conroy 9-5 M Cannon	–

Evens on Perseat, 3 to 1 agst Kilkerran, 5 Ebbing Tide, 10 Falster, 20 each Theale, Silchester.	5 to 4 on McCrankie, 4 to 1 Moon, 11 to 2 Skill, 10 each Lal Lal, Acrefield.	15 to 8 on Conroy, 4 to 1 agst Aureus, 100 to 9 Brechin, 100 to 8 Faversham, 20 others.
	Won by half a length; three-parts of a length.	Won a neck, a head.
Won a head; three quarters of a length.	Winner sold to Mr F R Hunt 200gns.	

The Final Meeting – Stockbridge Racecourse 1898
Tuesday 5th July, 1898
The Bibury Club Meeting

Hampshire Stakes of £468 for 3-y-o (1m)

576 Orpah 8-9
M Cannon **1**
552 Leisure Hour 8-12
Robinson **2**
482 Petty France 8-2
Allsopp **3**

7 to 4 on Orpah,
5 to 2 Leisure Hour,
8 Petty France.

Won half a length;
four lengths.

Houghton Selling Welter Plate of £100 (1m)

541 Kenwyn 5y
11-11 Mr Paget **1**
527 Bank-martin
3y 10-10
Mr Lushington **2**
Shrewd 3y 10-1
Capt Bewicke **3**
541 Ben Armine
4y 12-0
Mr H T Barclay **4**
457 Gribou 5y 11-11
Ld Cowley –
353 Silent Watch 4y
11-1 Mr Stacey –
573 Bantry Bay 4y
11-7 Mr Walker –

2 to 1 Shrewd,
3 Bank-martin,
5 Gribou,
8 Kenwyn and Ben
Armine.

Won a length;
three-parts of a length.
Winner sold to Mr W.
G. Stevens 190gns.

Fullerton Handicap of £195 (6f)

573 Red Virgin 4y 7-9
N Robinson **1**
381 Queen's Wake 4y
7-4 K Cannon **2**
600 Privado 4y 7-1
H Luke jnr **3**
554 Tartar 6y 9-4
Mr G Thursby **4**
565* Bobbie 3y 6-9
Purkis **5**
479 Horatia 3y 6-5
Dunn –
554 Gay Lumley 3y
7-7 Allsopp –
457 Florist 5y 7-7
S Loates –
436* Kleon 3y 7-2
Scourst –
580 King Tartar
5y 6-9 J Hunt –

4 to 1 Gay Lumley,
9 to 2 Tartar,
5 Red Virgin,
100-15 Privado,
7 King Tartar and
10 Queen's Wake.
Won by half a length;
3 lengths.

Bibury Stakes [Handicap] of £251 (1m 4f)

Cliviger 5y 11-10
Mr Thursby **1**
540* Bouncing Lad 3y
10-0 Mr Paget **2**
592 Nouveau Riche
5y 12-4 Mr Owen **3**
82 Somatose 4y 10-13
Ld Cowley **4**
603 Butter 4y 12-5
Ld Cholmondeley –
542* Palaver 4y 11-9
Mr Barclay –

11 to 4 Nouveau
Riche,
100 to 30 Bouncing
Lad and Butter,
7 Palaver, 8 Cliviger,
and
10 Somatose.

Won three parts of a
length; same.

Champagne Stakes of £340 for 2-y-o (Ab. 5f)

571 Quassia 8-9 M Cannon	1
466 Boucan 8-12 Allsopp	2
578* North Britain 9-8 K Cannon	3
425 Sidelight 8-9 N Robinson	4
Rigolet 8-12 S Loates	5
553 Knickerbocker 9-l Buet	–
497 Silver Thames 8-11 T Loates	–

9 to 4 Quassia,
7 to 2 North Britain,
4 Silver Thames,
6 Sidelight,
100 to 14 Boucan.

Won two lengths; a length and a half.

National Hunt Flat Race [Selling] of £97 (2m)

510 Miss Cristo a 12-7 Mr Hobson	1
500* Burnett 6y 12-7 Mr G S. Davis	2
510 Vel Vel 5y 12-3 Mr Lushington	3
Warrington a 12-7 Ld Cholmondeley	–
375* Miss Dolly II a 12-7 Mr Paget	–
539 Draconic a 12-7 Mr H.Owen	disq

evens Draconic,
5 Burnett and
Warrington, 100 to 8
Miss Cristo and Vel
Vel.

Won six lengths,
a length and a half.

Draconic came in
third, but was
disqualified for going
the wrong side of a
post.

Winner sold to Mr
Reid Walker 120gns

Bibury Club Junior Home-bred Stakes of £225 10s for 2y old. (Abt. 5f)

Loandal 8-1 T Loates	1
Forse 9-5 J Watts	2
330 Torpilleur 8-9 S Loates	3
Ruddle 8-4 Allsopp	–
Sir Paridel 8-0 M Cannon	–

evens Loendal,
5 to 2 Torpilleur,
4 Sir Paridel,
10 Forse and Ruddle.

Won a length and a
half;
a neck.

Wednesday 6th July, 1898
Stockbridge Meeting

Johnstone Plate (H'cap) of £100 (1m)

596 Cyrenian 4y 7-13
Madden   **1**
502 Simbre 5y 7-11
Robinson   **2**
457 Tight Rope
6y 6-9 Dunn   **3**
525 Milanyl 3y 6-12
C Cannon   **4**
577 Maria III a 7-12
Scourst   **5**
566 Switch 3y 6-7
Purkis   **6**
539* Maltravers a 8-7
Allsopp   –
467 Bobbie Burns 3y
7-7 S.Loates   –
565 Invermay 3y 7-0
B Lynham   –
339 Bonnie Prince
Charley
3y 6-10 H Luke   –

13 to 8 Cyrenian,
5 Tight Rope,
7 Simbre,
8 Maltravers.

Won a length,
four lengths.

Bonnie Prince Charlie
was left at the post.

Scurry Welter Plate of £100 (5f)

Newmarket a 11-10
Mr H Owen   **1**
573 Durrington 4y
11-0 Capt Bewicke **2**
540 Dalemore 3y
11-8 Mr Coventry **3**
488 Wagram 4y
11-10 Mr G.Paget **4**
597 Kilgrian 4y 11-8
Mr Lushington **5**
483 Peopleton 6y
11-9 Mr Barclay **6**
592* Bob White 5y
12-11 Mr Moore   –
572 Rowan Berry
4y 12-5
Mr A Schwabe   –
608 Red Virgin
4y 12-4
Mr G S Davies   –
565 Rodbourne
5y 11-11
Mr Withington   –
527 Monks Eleigh 5y
11-6 Capt Yardley –
California 5y 11-6
Mr Stacey   –

4 to 1 Dalemore,
5 Kilgrian,
11 to 2 Red Virgin,
6 Monks Eleigh and
Bob White,
8 Durrington,
10 Newmarket.

Won by a neck;
three-parts of a length.

Mottisfont Plate [Selling] of £185 for 2-y-o (5f)

540 Dormant 8-7
Allsopp   **1**
423 Glen-Choran 8-7
Rickaby   **2**
564 Till 8-4
S Loates   **3**
468 Larky 8-4
K Cannon   –

3 to 1 on Dormant,
5 Glen-Choran,
10 Till and Larky.

Won a head:
three lengths.

Winner sold to Mr R
H Combe 260gs.

Stockbridge Cup of £290. (6f)

554 Hips and Haws
4y 9-6 M.Cannon **1**
481 Edmee 2y 6-7
Purkis   **2**

6 to 4 on Hips and
Haws.

Won two lengths.

Andover Stakes (H'cap) of £170 (1m)

343* Morello a 11-9
Ld Cowley   1
467 Cyrard 3y 10-7
Mr Thursby   2
550 St. Maur
3y 10-10
Capt Bewicke   3
608 Ben Armine 4y
11-0 Mr Barclay   4
608 Somatose
4y 10-10
Mr Lushington   –
Horse Gill 3y 10-1
Mr Walker   –

2 to 1 Morello,
5 to 2 Cyrard,
7 to 2 St. Maur,
7 Somatose,
10 Horse Gill and Ben
Armine.

Won easily three
lengths;
same.

Danebury Plate [Selling] of £100 (5f)

240 g. by Radius-
Catterina
8-9 E Hunt   1
599* Baydon 8-12
S Loates   2
576 Sheppertonn 8-12
N Robinson   3
469* Acadian 8-12
Mr Thursby   4
581 Viburnum 8-9
Rickaby   5
483 Myrtleberry 8-12
K Cannon   6
c. by Fernandoz-
Rentless
8-12 M Cannon   –
465 c. by Lord Lorne-
Bengaline 8-12
W Freemantle   –
426 Timpout 8-9
O Madden   –
476 Barney 8-9
Allsopp   –
599 Saucer 8-9
Purkis   –
Coral Strand 8-4
C.Cannon   –

9 to 2 Viburnum,
5 Barney,
6 Catterina g., and
Myrtleberry,
7 Acadian, and
100 to 8 Shepperton
and Baydon.

Won by two lengths;
four lengths.

Winner bought in
710gns.

Beaufort H'cap Plate of £281 (1m 4f)

571 Harvest Money
5y 7-4 O Madden   1
555 Rampion 5y 7-12
K Cannon   2
600 Little Champion
3y 6-9 Chapman   3
438* Teufel 5y 8-13
M Cannon   –
Rizzio II 3y 6-7
B Lynham   –

7 to 4 Harvest
Money,
2 Rampion,
3 Teufel,
10 Little Champion
and Rizzio II.

Won by a length and a
half; six lengths.

Stockbridge Foal Stakes of £277 for 2-y-o (5f)

653 Flying Fox 9-5
M Cannon   1
482 No Trumps 8-8
Rickaby   2

9 to 4 on Flying Fox.

Won a length.

Thursday 7th July, 1898
Stockbridge Meeting

Broughton Selling Welter H'cap of £100 (6f)

609 Kilgrian 4y 11-5
Mr G S Davies   1
577 Bar Of Gold
4y 11-12
Capt C Bewicke   2
577* Affectation 5y
11-9 Mr Stacey   3
534* Poklad 4y 11-3
Mr Grenfell   4
608 Bantry Bay 4y
10-7 Mr Walker   5
Scrubbs 4y 11-3
Mr Hobson   –
540 Athcliath 5y 11-4
Mr Barclay   –
436 Lady Cricketer 4y
10-11 Mr Paget   –
565 Cleg 4y 10-7
Capt Yardley   –
578 Beauchief 3y 10-7
Mr Lushington   –

7 to 4 on Bar of Gold,
4 Beauchief,
8 Kilgrian,
100 to 7 Affectation.

Won by a length and a half;
three-parts of a length.

Winner sold to
Mr W T Robinson
210gns.

Alington Plate [H'cap] of £460 (1m)

592* Dynamo 5y 8-5
Rickaby   1
610* Hips and Haws
4y 9-0 M Cannon   2
575* Addendum 3y
7-4 K Cannon   3
602 Duamia 4y 7-7
S.Loates   4

11 to 8 Addendum,
9 to 4 Dynamo,
100 to 30 Hips and
Haws, 7 Duamia.

Won a length;
two lengths.

Wallop Plate [Selling H'cap] of £100 (1m)

608 Silent Watch 4y
11-6 Mr Stacey   1
678 Red Coral
5y 11-12
Mr G S Davies   2
610 Ben Armine 4y
11-3 Mr Barclay   3
642 Upper Cut
4y 11-10
Mr H Ripley   –

7 to 4 Red Coral,
2 Upper Cut,
100 to 30 Ben Armine,
6 Silent Watch.

Won easily by two lengths;
a neck.

Winner sold to
Mr W H Moore
450gns.

Hurstbourne Stakes of £622 for 2-y-o. (5f)

Lady Ogle 8-6
S Loates   1
593 Manners 9-1
J Watts   2
276 Aslingdon 9-0
Allsopp   3
603 Mark For'ard 9-0
M Cannon   –
698 f by Morion-
Lady Yardley
8-11 Madden   –

15 to 8 Mark For'ard,
2 Aslingdon,
9 to 2 Lady Ogle,
7 Manners and Lady
Yardley filly.

Won by two lengths;
a head.

All-aged Plate [Selling] of £100 (5f)

468 Telesinus a 9-7
Madden   1
478 Dancer 5y 9-7
Purkis   2
581* Bouthillier a 9-7
Mr Lushington   3
481 Entrisence 4y 9-4
M Cannon   –
595 Blue Smoke 3y
8-11 E Hunt   –
Gralloch 3y 8-11
W Freemantle   –
Moonwave 3y 8-6 §
C Cannon   –
469 Dynamic 3y 8-11
Mr Thursby   –

5 to 4 Blue Smoke,
7 to 4 Entrisence,
7 Dancer,
100 to 8 Telesinus,
100 to 7 Bouthillier

Won by three-parts of
a length;
three lengths.

Longstock Plate of £100 (1 m)

611* Dynamo 5y
10-10 Rickaby   1
552 Heckler 3y 9-7
M Cannon   2
578 Allglow 3y 8-2
N Robinson   3

11 to 10 Dynamo,
9 to 4 Heckler,
5 to 2 Allglow.

Won easily by two
lengths;
six lengths.

Match of £100 (5f)

466 Wolf 's Hope 2y
9-2 M Cannon   1
594 Doddington 2y
9-2 J Watts   2

100 to 30 on Wolf 's
Hope.

Won by a length and a
half.

End of meeting

REFERENCES

1. Penelope Stokes. *Free Rein, Racing in Berkshire and Beyond 1700-1905*. (2005). p.12.
2. as above p.19.
3. as above p. 94.
4. William Scambler. *Memories of the Pentons*. (2006). p.15.
5. Stokes. *Free Rein*. p.113.
6. John Cheny. *Historical List of all horse-matches run, and of all plates and prizes run for in England*. (1725-1750). [1742]
7. William Day and Alfred J. Day. *The Racehorse in Training*. (1880 and 1925). p.183.
8. *Andover Advertiser*, 24 June 1870.
9. Stokes. *Free Rein*. pp. 26, 51.
10. *The British Turf, and the Men who have made it. Being an Historical and Contemporary Work on Racing in the British Isles from its earliest inception to the present day*. p.97.
11. Stokes. *Free Rein*. p.54.
12. 'Borderer'. 'The English Race Courses' in *Outing* no.16 (1902) p.106.
    Note: *Outing* was a late 19th - early 20th cent. magazine covering a variety of sporting activities. It began publication in 1882 as *The Wheelman* and had four title changes before ceasing publication in 1923.
13. Letter from J. Ernest Pain to Lord Warwick, offering his house for the Stockbridge Races; written from Westover, Andover, 28 April 1893. Warwickshire CRO, CR1886/Box 832/69.
14. Tessa Lecomber. *The Barker-Mill Story*. (2000). pp.46-53.
15. Rachel Vorspan. *Rational Recreation, and the Law: The Transformation of Popular Urban Leisure in Victorian England*. (U.C. Berkley 1967).
16. Lecomber. *The Barker-Mill Story*. p.53.
17. *Andover Advertiser*, 8th July 1898.
18. Melville T.H. Child. *Farms, Fairs and Felonies*. (1967).
19. Valerie Martin. *This is Findon Village*. [webpage ref: www.findonvillage.com]
20. *Oxford Dictionary of National Biography*. J. Barham Day, by Emma Eadie.
21. Sir Reginald Graham. *Foxhunting Recollections*. (1907).
22. W.H. Jacob. *Hampshire at the Turn of the Twentieth Century*. (1905).

BIBLIOGRAPHY

Andover Advertiser, newspaper, various dates.

Dorothy Beresford. *Nether Wallop in Hampshire.* (1973)

Robin J. Brooks. *Hampshire Airfields' in the Second World War.* (Countryside Books, 1996)

Lord W. George H. Cavendish Bentinck, papers of, in the Portland (Welbeck) Collection at Nottingham University and online catalogue.

Census Records, 1871, 1881 and 1891.

John Cheny. *Historical List of all horse-matches run, and of all plates and prizes run for in England. (1725-1750)*

Melville T.H.Child. *Farms, Fairs and Felonies.* (1967)

J.Daniels, A.Dougall and D.Livermore. *The History of Houghton and Bossington.* (2000)

William Day. *Reminiscences of the Turf.* (Bentley & Son, 1886) *Turf Celebrities I Have Known.* (White, 1891)

William Day and Alfred J. Day. *The Racehorse in Training.* (Cassell, 1880 and 1925)

Hubert Earney. 'Danebury Dynasty' in *Hampshire Magazine.* (March 1978)

Sir Reginald Graham. *Foxhunting Recollections.* (London, 1907)

Charles C. F. Greville, ed. Henry Reeve. *A Journal of the Reign of Queen Victoria from 1837-1852.* (1885) vol.III, pp.222-234. [Article from Greville's Journal, 28 Sept. 1848]

Hampshire Chronicle, newspaper, various dates.

June Harris. 'Victorian Danebury: a family memoir' in *Hampshire Magazine* (January 1993)

Rosalind Hill. *A Short History of Stockbridge and its Churches.* (1963)

W. H. Jacob. *Hampshire at the Turn of the Twentieth Century.* (Pike, 1905)

James Lawton. *Lester Piggott.* (Coronet Books, 1980)

Tessa Lecomber. *The Barker-Mill Story.* (2000)

Valerie Martin. *This is Findon Village.*

Vic Mitchell and Keith Smith. *Andover to Southampton.* (Middleton Press, 1990)

D. H. Moutray Read. *Highways and Byways in Hampshire.* (Macmillan. 1908)

The Oxford Dictionary of National Biography. [for J. Barham Day]

Mary Pollock. 'The History of Stockbridge Races'; a talk given to the Somborne Society, 28 November 2001.

Marigold Routh. *Amport. The Story of a Hampshire Parish.* (1986)

Salisbury Journal, newspaper, various dates.

William Scambler. *Memories of the Pentons.* (2006)

Barry Shurlock. *Red Guide Hampshire.* (Waymark Publications, 1989)

John Spaul. *Andover. An Historical Portrait.* (Andover Local Archives Comm. 1978)

Penelope Stokes. *Free Rein. Racing in Berkshire and Beyond 1700-1905.* (Newbury, 2005)

Derek J. Tempero. *They Simply Stole to Live.* (Holmes & Sons, c.2000)

Martin Thornhill. *Explorers' Hampshire.* (Skeffington & Son, 1952)

David Underdown. *Start of Play. Cricket and Culture in Eighteenth-Century England.* (Penguin Books, 2000)

Rachel Vorspan. *Rational Recreation and the Law: The Transformation of Popular Urban Leisure in Victorian England.* (U.C.Berkley, 1967)

William White. *Directory of Hampshire and the Isle of Wight. (1859)*

GLOSSARY OF TERMS AND ABBREVIATIONS

2yo	Two year old horse
Alw	Type of Race – allowance race
b.c.	bay colt
banker	A term used to describe a good thing, that is a horse that should win.
bay	Colour of horse varying from yellowish tan (light bay) to brown or dark, rich shade of mahogany (sometimes listed as dark bay or brown) with black points - black mane, tail and shadings of black low on the legs.
blackleg	Early derogatory name for a bookmaker (turf accountant) from lowly origins, so named as they wore top boots because they could not afford stockings. They were sometimes known as turf swindlers
c	colt
c.g.	colt gelding
ch.c	Chestnut colt
chestnut	Colour of horse varying from light, washy yellow to dark liver colour, between which comes red, gold and liver shades. A chestnut never has black points, mane or tail
claiming race	Race in which horses are entered subject to claim for a specified price.
Clerk of the Course	The person responsible for the overall management of a racecourse during the raceday
Clm	Type of Race – claim race
colt	Male horse under 5 years of age
colours	Shirts or 'silks' worn by jockeys to identify a horse to a particular owner
f	filly
filly	Female horse up to and including the age of 4
ft.	Abbreviation for track condition – fast
Furlong	1/8 of a mile. Equal to 220 yards or 200 metres
g	gelding
gd	Abbreviation for track condition – good
gelding	Castrated male horse
g s	guineas (21 shillings or £1.05)
h.	Thoroughbred age 5 or older
hand	Four inches. Unit used in measuring height of horses from withers to ground
hd	head
head	A margin between horses. One horse leading another by the length of his head
L&SWR	London and South West Railway company
length	Length of a horse from nose to tail, about 8 feet. Also distance between horses in a race
Mare	Female horse aged 5 years or over
Mdm	Type of Race – maiden race
ra	Abbreviation for track condition – rain affected
selling race	A claiming race
sl	Abbreviation for track condition - slow
sovs.	sovereigns (20 shillings or £1.00)

stake	A race (usually a feature race) for which owner must pay up a fee to run a horse. The fees can be for nominating, maintaining eligibility, entering and starting, to which the track adds more money to make up the total purse. Some stakes races are by invitation and require no payment or fee
Stk	Type of Race – stakes race
Str	Type of Race – starter
Thoroughbred	A horse whose family tree can be traced to horses registered in the 'General Stud Book'
wf	Abbreviation for track condition – wet fast
ws	Abbreviation for track condition – wet slow
wta	Winner Takes All - a winner receiving all the purse or stakes

INDEX